A 2024-2029 Strategic Plan for Securing Black American (Afrodescendant) Reparations

Brooks Robinson, Ph.D.

BlackEconomics.org
P. O. Box 8848
Honolulu, HI 96380-8848
https://www.BlackEconomics.org
BlackEconomics@BlackEconomics.org

Acknowledgement

We offer our deepest and sincerest thanks to Black American (Afrodescen-dant) ancestors who comprehended the value of Reparations; especially those who worked purposely and diligently to obtain Reparations.

We thank the Universal Creator within for aligning us with our ancestors' efforts and for the opportunity to help identify a strategic plan that ensures receipt of Reparations.

We extend heartfelt gratitude to Long-Term Strategic Plan Panelists and to members of the Team of Reparations Experts that was assembled by the Afrodescendant Nation during 2023. They all helped expand our knowledge of Reparations.

Contemplations

"…I agree with everything my brother said about revolutionaryism. [But] Who fishes? Who knows how to fish? Hands down. Who knows how to hunt? Less hands. Hands down. Who shoots on a regular basis, meaning once or twice weekly? Hands down. Now you see how many hands. Who farms or grows their own food right now? Hands down. You ain't ready to oppose nothing…"

"Killer Mike" speaking during the 2016 All Black National Convention in Atlanta, Georgia. (https://www.youtube.com/watch?v=Bl1XoK3juVs, Ret. 043024).

**"Sometimes We Can Choose Our Timing.
Sometimes Timing Chooses Us!"**

Adapted from a statement from the late Sen. Eward Kennedy (D-MA) during a 2007 conversation with then Sen. Barack Obama (D-IL); John Farrell (2023). "Ted Kennedy Passes the Torch." American Heritage; https://www.americanheritage.com/ted-kennedy-passes-torch (Ret. 051224).

"Let My People Go" *Exodus* 5:1

"…They Shall Come Out with Great Possessions." *Gensis* 15:14

Summary

This nine-chapter pocketbook uses these ripe times to urge an amplified surge in pursuit of Black American (Afrodescendant) Reparations. It provides foundational information for leveling the conversation field on the Reparations topic. It offers a concise strategic plan for securing Reparations in the near term; yet it is flexible and easily adaptable for meeting longer term requirements. It vanquishes the three traditional economic arguments against extending Reparations to Black Americans: i.e., Reparations will be debt increasing, tax increasing, and inflation inducing. Most importantly, it proposes a novel and pain-free method for paying the Reparations claim.

JEL Codes: H59, J15, O23, P11, Z13

Table of Contents

List of Acronyms

ADN	Afrodescendant Nation
AI	Artificial Intelligence
BEA	Bureau of Economic Analysis
CBC	Congressional Black Caucus
CBO	Congressional Budget Office
CNBC	Conference of National Black Churches
CSRP	Comprehensive Strategic Reparations Plan
FED	Federal Reserve Board
FY	Fiscal Year
GAO	Government Accountability Office
IBW21	Institute of the Black World 21st Century
ITC	International Theological Center
LFNOI	Lost Found Nation of Islam
MMT	Modern Monetary Theory
NAACP	National Association for the Advancement of Colored People
NAARC	National African American Reparations Commission
NAN	National Action Network
NBA	National Bar Association
NEA(1)	National Economic Association
NEA (2)	National Education Association
NMA	National Medical Association
NRC	National Reparations Council
NOI	Nation of Islam
NUL	National Urban League
OMB	Office of Management and Budget
RC	Reparation Commision
UN	United Nations

Chapter 1: Introduction

Most Black Americans (Afrodescendants) have rightly or wrongly placed economic concerns atop our agendas. The "economic inequality" topic is at the forefront of discussions about race in America. Nearly by definition this means that discussions go directly to—or meander to—Reparations. These Reparations discussions can be broad and nebulous, or they can focus on single, multiple, and specific concerns. The following are the types of core questions that are entertained during Reparations discussions. What are Reparations? Why should Reparations be paid? What is the Reparations bill? Who is(are) the culpable party(ies)? In which form(s) should Reparations be extended—if they are ever extended? Who should receive Reparations payments?

This concise volume provides answers to the foregoing questions, but it also serves as a rich resource on other important aspects of Reparations. This volume's most important contributions to the Reparations literature and conversation are embodied in Chapters 6 and 7. They address the most fundamental, yet least discussed Reparations-related questions. Cataloguing justifications for Reparations and estimating definitive Reparations amounts are, no doubt, important and essential first and second steps on a **path** that may lead to Reparations logically. However, these seemingly very important steps may be characterized as "putting the cart before the horse." To rightly put the horse before the cart, Black Americans (Afrodescendants) require a systematically and strategically planned **path** so that we are all crystal-clear about how to undertake this enormously important Reparations journey and ensure that we receive Reparations when the journey concludes.

We will not overlook here, however, the importance of Chapter 8, which details a strategy that the US Government can adopt to extend Reparations to Black Americans (Afrodescendants). Certain Reparations scholars have argued that funds for Reparations can be derived by reducing expenditures in selected Federal Government programs. At the same time, many who oppose or reject the idea that Reparations should be extended to Black Americans (Afrodescendants) raise the following red flags: They argue that Reparations will be tax increasing, budget busting, and inflation inducing. Chapter 8 reveals a strategy that vanquishes this opposition.

In the Spring of 2023 as part of an Afrodescendant Nation (ADN) planning effort to organize an October 2023 Reparations Convention in Atlanta, a question surfaced about the existence of an overarching plan to secure Black American (Afrodescendant) Reparations. The answer came that unlike the *Long-Term Strategic Plan for Black America*, there was no such overarching strategic plan for obtaining Reparations.[1] Hence, the ADN decided to prepare a Comprehensive Strategic Reparations Plan (CSRP).

Calls went out to numerous important Black American (Afrodescendant) organizations, institutions, and individuals engaged in the ongoing Reparations fight to join the ADN's effort to craft a CSRP. It turned out that almost all parties called were too busy with their own and independent, idiosyncratic, and fragmentary effort that they could/did not allocate time or other required resources to the ADN's CSRP project. This outcome indicated, in part, that the importance of developing a plan to coordinate and guide efforts for complex projects like the fight for Black American (Afrodescendant) Reparations is not well comprehended. If the truth be known, the ADN, too, was quite shy of time and other resources to devote to the CSRP project. Several virtual meetings were organized, but little more than a scantily populated CSRP outline was developed before the October 2023 Atlanta Reparations Convention. A refined version of that outline was floated at the convention along with a request for comments and resources to help develop the plan. Unfortunately, little interest emerged in developing such an essential planning document.

During the early months of 2024, the ADN continued mainly internal efforts to develop the CSRP, but little progress was made. In early April 2024, an ADN collaborating organization, BlackEconomics.org, renewed a commitment to assist with developing the CSRP. BlackEconomics.org pointed out that the comprehensive nature and long-term time horizon that the CSRP was expected to span cast the document as too formidable to tackle. So much so that it served as a deterrent to progress. Even large groups find elephant eating to be problematic. BlackEconomics.org agreed to restructure the project and prepare the current volume by streamlining the initially intended coverage and addressing only the most essential aspects of Reparations, including a strategic plan for securing Reparations. BlackEconomics.org worked hurriedly during April and the first half of May to complete this volume so that it could be released selectively to participants at an ADN Washington, DC Reparations Convention during May 17-19, 2024.

The volume should be viewed as a basic tool for navigating the Black American (Afrodescendant) Reparations journey successfully in the immediate to near term. At the same time, it can and may be revised easily in the future to extend the time horizon and to augment or expand strategic details to ensure a successful Reparations journey.

---

[1] Long-Term Strategic Plan Panel (2023). *Long-Term Strategic Plan for Black America.* Long-Term Strategic Plan Panelists. Honolulu. https://www.ltspfba.org/LTSP/fin_ltspfba_071223.pdf (Ret. 051224).

As already noted, the most meaningful and unique information in this volume appears in Chapters 6 and 7. These chapters expand on and operationalize a conceptual framework that was embedded in an idea popularized by long-time Reparations warrior, Kamm Howard, who envisioned a mainly political path to Reparations.[2] Of course, the volume also provides concise answers to the aforementioned and common topical questions that surface in everyday conversations about Reparations.

The volume can serve as a "pocketbook" at one's fingertips as a ready reference on Black American (Afrodescendant) Reparations. Most importantly, the volume should generate excited anticipation about receiving Reparations in the not-too-distant future as the title and strategic plan timetable show 2024-2029 as the suggested period for reaching this lofty goal. Reparations by 2029 may seem overly optimistic—even a pipe dream. However, if one does not ask, then one does not receive. The squeaky wheel gets the grease. If we do not try, then we are assured of failure. Therefore, all Black Americans (Afrodescendants) are urged to adopt the path set forth herein for transporting us from today's gloomy *status quo* to the joy that will envelop us on that day when Reparations appear to brighten our way.

---

[2] Kamm Howard is a long-time N'COBRA (National Coalition for Black Reparations in America) leader and advocate, who, *inter alia*, founded a new Reparations organization in 2022, Reparations United that he directs: https://reparationsunited.org/our-director/ (Ret. 041524).

Chapter 2: Definition of Reparations

It is almost always appropriate to define terms when first engaging a topic. On the other hand, one might think that it would **not** be important or necessary to provide a definition for a term as popular as Reparations. But such a thought would be misguided. It is a well-documented fact that social media can be a voluminous and powerful source of misinformation. Also, it is common knowledge that many Black Americans (Afrodescendants), especially our youth, use social media as their primary source of news and information. Hence, while we will not tarry long in defining Reparations, we provide definitions for Reparations from six well-known and relevant sources that can be assessed and interpreted in light of their stature.

We begin with the United Nation's definition of Reparations as the definitive source for international discussions of the topic. N'COBRA (National Coalition of Blacks for Reparations in America), the oldest Black American (Afrodescendant) organization solely dedicated to securing Reparation developed its own definition as a starting point at the onset of its operations in 1987. In 2015, the Institute of the Black World 21st Century (IBW21) announced the formation of the National African American Reparations Commission (NAARC), which is composed of eminent scholars and Reparations experts. The NAARC's definition of Reparations is provided. The definition offered by the most respected and cited economist Reparations scholar team (Darity and Mullen) is provided. We convey the definition given in the most detailed state government document produced to reflect analyses of the case for, costs of, and proposals for Reparations—the *California Task Force to Study and Develop Reparations Proposals for African Americans*. Finally, we present a succinct and comprehensive definition of Reparations from the National Institute for Reparations that appears in Reginal Muhammad's *Reparations Declaration*.

United Nations

Section IX.15 of United Nations (UN) General Assembly Resolution 60/147, which was adopted on 16 December 2005 states:[3]

---

[3] See United Nation's General Assembly Resolution 60/147 (2006), "Basic Principles and Guidelines on the Right to a Remedy and Reparation for Victims of Gross Violations of International Human Rights Law and Serious Violations of International Humanitarian Law." https://www.ohchr.org/sites/default/files/2021-08/N0549642.pdf (Ret. 041524).

Adequate, effective and prompt reparation is intended to promote justice by redressing gross violations of international human rights law or serious violations of international humanitarian law. Reparation should be proportional to the gravity of the violations and the harm suffered. In accordance with its domestic laws and international legal obligations, a State shall provide reparation to victims for acts or omissions which can be attributed to the State and constitute gross violations of international human rights law or serious violations of international humanitarian law. In cases where a person, a legal person, or other entity is found liable for reparation to a victim, such party should provide reparation to the victim or compensate the State if the State has already provided reparation to the victim. [p. 7]

Section IX.19-23 of the Resolution identifies five principles with which to comport when developing and dispensing Reparations: (i) Restitution; (ii) Compensation; (iii) Rehabilitation: (iv) Satisfaction; and (v) Guarantees of non-Repetition. [pp. 7-8]

N'COBRA

The nearly 40-year-long effort by N'COBRA rests on the following definition (explanation) for Reparations:[4]

Reparations is a process of repairing, healing and restoring a people injured because of their group identity and in violation of their fundamental human rights by governments or corporations. Those groups that have been injured have the right to obtain from the government or corporation responsible for the injuries that which they need to repair and heal themselves. In addition to being a demand for justice, it is a principle of international human rights law. As a remedy, it is similar to the remedy for damages in domestic law that holds a person responsible for injuries suffered by another when the infliction of the injury violates domestic law. [p. 1]

---

[4] This definition appears in a 2004 document entitled, "Reparations and the National Coalition of Blacks for Reparations in American (N'COBRA): An Information Sheet." https://ncobra.org/resources/pdf/Information%20Sheet%20Master%20-%20NCOBRA.pdf (Ret. 041524).

NAARC

The NAARC provides two important statements on its Internet website, which can be construed to constitute its definition (description) of Reparations:[5]

> The goal of full reparations is to wipe out all consequences of harms committed by a government. To meet the standard of full reparations, there are five areas of intended outcomes: Cessation, Assurance and Guarantees of Non-Repetition, Restitution and Repatriation, Compensation, Satisfaction, and Rehabilitation. As such, reparations must repair beyond monetary gain, it must dismantle the institution structures that continue to perpetuate white supremacy.

> *Comprehensive reparations* are expansive and focus on redressing crimes against humanity endured by Black communities (people of African descent) due to chattel slavery, U.S. Apartheid system (Jim Crow), the current period of systemic racism, and their on-going impact. Also, Comprehensive Reparations focus on repairing Black communities with forward-thinking initiatives that safeguard the future of Black America. Comprehensive Reparations are holistic and include remedies for reparations based on a range of harm.

Darity and Mullen

The authors of the 2020 volume *From Here to Equality: Reparations for Black Americans in the Twenty-First Century* and many other submissions on Reparations provide a concise definition of the term in the just-mentioned book's Introduction:[6]

> "Reparations are a program of acknowledgment, redress, and closure for a grievous injustice. Where African Americans are concerned, the grievous injustices that make the case for reparations include slavery, legal

---

[5] These NAARC statements appear at the following Internet address: https://reparationscomm.org/naarc-news/press-releases/comprehensive-reparations-for-black-america-primer/ (Ret. 041524).
[6] William Darity, Jr. and A. Kirsten Mullen (2020). *From Here to Equality: Reparations for Black Americans in the Twenty-First Century.* The University of North Carolina Press. Chapel Hill.

segregation (Jim Crow), and ongoing discrimination and stigmatization." (p. 2).

California Task Force

The *California Task Force to Study and Develop Reparation Proposals for African Americans: Final Report* reflects adoption of the UN General Assembly's principles established in Resolution 60/147 (mentioned above) with which to analyze Black American (Afrodescendant) injuries imposed or permitted by the State of California that warrant Reparations (p. 512).

National Reparations Institute

Prof. Reginald Muhammad provides a most concise, yet comprehensive definition of Reparation:

> Complete Reparations: The process by which a nation of people is provided with the means to repair and restore their condition, achieve complete decolonization, and make themselves whole through the ability to self-govern, self-sustain and self-defend, with their own independent land mass, economy, education, culture, and high civilization.[7]

These just-given six definitions are provided to fulfill this volume's commitment to serve as a ready reference on selected aspects of Reparations. It is transparent that definitions of Reparations can vary while carrying similar meanings, intents, themes, and requirements. It is important that these definitions be presented because they help level the knowledge playing field when discussions of Reparations arise. Also, as noted at the outset of this chapter, it is simply a sound practice to define terms when commencing exploration of topics—especially topics as complex and as important as Black Americans (Afrodescendant) Reparations.

---

[7] Reginald Muhammad (2023). *The Reparations Declaration: A Qualitative and Quantitative Blueprint for Black Redress* (Expanded Edition). National Reparations Institute. Atlanta. (p. 1). https://www.nationalreparationsinstitute.org/product-page/soft-copy-the-national-reparations-declaration (Ret. 043024).

Chapter 3: Why Reparations?

Warning! This chapter's topic question is addressed from a philosophical/religious/spiritual vantage point. The author is empowered to adopt this perspective because Black Americans (Afrodescendants) still retain a strong connection to our African roots that grew deep over eons in a soil rich with philosophic/religious/spiritual traditions.

We begin by acknowledging that the most important interrogative for humans is "why." When asked and answered exhaustively, one can arrive at the crux of matters. Like the study of history, answers to a complete set of why questions are sufficient to reward all research.

In this case, whys about Black American Reparations takes one to the most inhumane and despicable treatment ever enacted by one human group against another. The unconscionable actions taken were motivated by greed, and they were justified using false contrivances about skin color.

Asking why carries one to the religious foundation of the US nation, and uncovers blatant hypocrisy of a claim on the one hand that God the Creator placed "man" on Earth as vicegerent and did not differentiate initially. The claim then pivots and differentiates White man/woman advantageously over Black, Brown, and Yellow men/women. The reason for this flip-flop is justified by one idiosyncratic event during the very long course of human history (the so-called "Hamitic Curse").[8] The hypocrisy reeks with injustice because even knowledge of Jesus the Christ—the greater atoner and reconciler—was insufficient to produce a path of redemption for non-Whites who are Black.

Asking why returns us to the hypocrisy of the US nation again because its founding fathers wrote in a fulcrum founding document "that all men are created equal" nearly 250 years ago.[9] Yet those words live as bitter, egregious, painfully injurious, and deadly lies in the hearts and minds of White Americans to this very day.

---

[8]The *Holy Bible's* book of *Genesis* 9:22-27 records the event mentioned in the text. Because Ham, Noah's son, is said to have viewed his father's nakedness and is then cursed by his father is the basis for the so-called "Hamitic Curse." Biblical genealogical lines assign Ham to the region known today as Northeastern Africa: Cush, Egypt, Put, and Canaan—a land of Black people. See *Genesis*: 10:6.

[9] The words in inverted commas are from the second paragraph of the *Declaration of Independence.*

One why will take you to Special Field Order 15 issued by General William Tecumseh Sherman, who seems to live up to the nobility of the namesake of his middle name (Native American Shawnee Tribal Chief and warrior Tecumseh).[10] However, big thieves and liars in the US Government reached down from Washington, DC and made Sherman out to be a liar by rescinding the "40 acres and mule" order, thereby denying newly freed slaves access to a reasonably fair start in life immediately following the Civil War.[11]

A near 100-year-later why will bring you to the 1954 *Brown vs. Board Topeka, Kansas* US Supreme Court case, and lies hidden in the words "with all deliberate speed" that were buried in the case's decision.[12]

Also, a similar near 100-year-later why will bring you to the 1964 Civil Rights Act and Title VII's Equal Employment Opportunity Commission (EEOC). The EEOC was created and tasked with ensuring the truth of America's economic fairness that could enable all men and women to acquire good jobs based on merit, and a decent and comfortable life for families using wages and salaries that were fair. The stated purpose of the EEOC was and is a huge lie because it has never been funded at a level even close to sufficient to fulfil its written mandate by enforcing discrimination laws.[13]

---

[10] See "Tecumseh." National Park Service. https://www.nps.gov/people/tecumseh.htm (Ret. 041824).

[11] Nadra Kareem Nittle (2024). "The Short-Lived Promise of '40 Acres and a Mule'." History.com. https://www.history.com/news/40-acres-mule-promise (Ret. 041824).

[12] "All deliberate speed" appears in the *Brown v. Board of Education, Topeka Kansas, 1954* US Supreme Court Decision. The specific quote comes from so-called Brown II, which was delivered in 1955. See *Brown v. Board of Education (1954)*. https://www.archives.gov/milestone-documents/brown-v-board-of-education#transcript (Ret. 043024).

[13] For fiscal year (FY) 2023, the EEOC reports that it began with 51,399 pending discrimination charges to resolve, received over 81,055 new charges, and ended the FY with 51,100 pending charges. This computes to 81,354 charges being addressed and resolved during the FY. However, these statistics reveal that new charges arise nearly as fast as pending charges are revolved; this remains the case 60 years after the Civil Rights Act of 1964. These results lead to the conclusion that the EEOC has not served as an effective deterrent to discrimination—especially discrimination based on race. See the EEOC's Annual Performance Report for FY 2023; https://www.eeoc.gov/2023-annual-performance-report#:~:text=Receiving%2081%2C055%20new%20discrimination%20charges,25%25%20from%20fiscal%20year%202022; (Ret. 043024).

Not only were these 100-year-later whys lies, but many more and even more horrific lies were planted and grew during that 100-year period.

The whys of Reparations will give you a flyby of lies about murders of Black American prophets including Medgar, Malcolm, Martin, and others that are so deceitful hidden that we may never know the truth.

Reparations whys will have you examining lies about a continuous flow of "bait and switch" and other deceitful strategies designed to keep Black Americans outside the nation's citizenship rights circle, while leveraging our minds and bodies as fodder for meritless production that destroys us individually and collectively. For example: (i) The rise of Affirmative Action followed by Bakke;[14] (ii) racial integration in education that morphed into resegregation;[15] (iii) urban renewal that featured destruction of our areas of influence and, later, gentrification;[16] (iv) myths about Black youths' inability to learn, when we know that our children are "learning machines;"[17] (v) a false war on drugs that was a chain of wealth-creating

---

[14] Richard Ford (2022). "Derailed by Diversity: The Supreme Court Has Watered Down Affirmative Action's Core Justification: Justice. *The Chronicle of Higher Education*.
https://www.chronicle.com/article/derailed-by-diversity (Ret. 050224).

[15] The National Center for Education Statistics (NCES) reports that, during 2019, 81.6% of Black American public elementary and secondary school students attended schools where over 50% of the students were non-White. See Table 216.50 of the *Direct of Education Statistics* from the US Department of Education, NCES (2022).

[16] The Joe Biden Administration's inclusion of a "Reconnecting Communities" component in its $1 trillion Infrastructure Bill is *prima facie* evidence of well-known outcomes associated with US Government actions. See "Fact Sheet: President Biden Announces Over $3 billion to Reconnect Communities That Have Been Left Behind and Divided by Transportation Infrastructure." https://www.whitehouse.gov/briefing-room/statements-releases/2024/03/13/fact-sheet-president-biden-announces-over-3-billion-to-reconnect-communities-that-have-been-left-behind-and-divided-by-transportation-infrastructure/ (Ret. 050224).

[17] It is common knowledge, extensively studied, and an often-cited fact that the educational performance of Black American (Afrodescendant) students is affected significantly by the race/ethnicity of their instructors. Simply put, students perform better when taught by same race/ethnicity instructors. Therefore, it is not that students are unable to learn, it is that students' learning is highly conditioned on their instructors. The term "learning machines" is attributable to our co-contributor at BlackEconomics.org, Lindsey "Rob" Robinson.

opportunities mainly for non-Blacks including illegal drug sales, sales of weapons, and illegal and unjust incarcerations to fill to overflowing the pockets of judges, attorneys, the police, jail and prison administrators and operators, and investors;[18] and (vi) most recently, partly contrived healthcare crises to, *inter alia*, test economic management prowess, newly available digital technologies, and strategies for social control.[19]

Some may argue that the foregoing whys are not germane to Black American (Afrodescendant) Reparations. They say that we seek Reparations as compensation for harms done—Whites to Blacks. The thought is that Reparations will serve as a highly respected atonement process. The most gracious and humane among Black Americans (Afrodescendants) may argue that Reparations as atonement will reconcile and save the nation's diverse races/ethnicities, facilitate healing, and give the nation a fighting chance at renewal and a righteous rebirth.

This is not to argue against the just-stated perspective. However, our response—which commences with "and" not "but"—is that no matter where we explore in written human history (especially in religious literatures), the story does not end until "wrongs" have been "righted" through the transformation or destruction of the people. The whys and lies highlighted above are simply intended to suggest that Black Americans' (Afrodescendants') current thrust for Reparations was and is motivated by Black American (Afrodescendant) prophets' truthful revelations and

---

[18] As a "proxy" for earnings of those benefitting from real growth of the US prison industrial complex, we use growth in total real government expenditures on the "Public Order and Safety" (POS) function. These data are reflected in the US Department of Commerce, Bureau of Economic Analysis's National Income and Product Account Table 3.15.3. Real Government Consumption Expenditures and Gross Investment by Function, Quantity Indexes (www.bea.gov, Ret. 050224). The table shows that from 1990 to 2022, growth in expenditures (in percentage terms) for POS ranked third among the nine functions presented. Expenditure growth for the POS function only lagged expenditures for the Health and Income Security functions.

[19] It is common knowledge that the Covid-19 Pandemic transformed life as we knew it with dramatically increased and intensified use of telecommunications to facilitate operations in virtual work environments. The impact continues today as "work from home" arrangements have emptied many office buildings and may trigger a financial crisis for those engaged in lending for commercial real estate. Also, certain locales have experienced a dramatic decline (other locales have witnessed increases) in their populations as workers, who are no longer tied to a location, have shifted to more amenable climatological zones.

visions. Not only that, but it is Black Americans' (Afrodescendants') duty to push these revelations and visions to their logical limits. In doing so, we help ensure that this stage of human history, too, reflects the righting of wrongs. More importantly, the "impossible" task that will have been achieved when Black Americans (Afrodescendants) receive Reparations will represent one of the greatest examples of religious faith and works in human history and a magnificent glorification of the Universal Creator, who is well-known for the power to make something extraordinarily wonderful out of absolutely nothing.

Humans have reached a point in world history where we have all that is required to return Earth to a pleasant paradise. But paradise cannot emerge or exist alongside evil. A popular saying is: "If you will lie, then you will steal; and if you will steal, then you will kill." Natural human morality disdains lies, theft, and murder. They are evil! The world should unify to expunge evil from the Earth and produce an opportunity for a return to paradise. Black Americans' (Afrodescendants') receipt of Reparations will mark the onset of a thorough crushing of lies, which is a starting point for ending evil.

Therefore, the most noble answer to the topic question "Why Reparations?" is to initiate Earth's renewal as a place of peace and paradise.

Chapter 4: Reparations From and For Whom?

Answers to this chapter's topic question are designed to help parameterize the parties engaged in the Black American (Afrodescendant) Reparations process. Answers are dispensed with certain guidance that promises to be important in determining whether efforts to secure Reparations will be successful. Also, for completeness, we will rip away potential Repairers' "crying towel" defenses against Reparations as efforts to secure Reparations intensify. Such crying towel defenses are the oldest "trick in the book," and are expected. They are endemic to those who exhibit a long and bloody history of feeding their greedy minds, bodies, and souls through the merciless exploitation of others.

For the record, Black Americans (Afrodescendants) are seeking Reparations from non-Black Americans. Do not be surprised that the previous statement does not conclude with the words "White Americans." There is no question that Whites' emergence from Europe was the onset of bad trouble for African and other non-White people the world over. Also, there is no doubt that the arrival of Africans as unlawful prisoners in the Americas and who were forced into chattel slavery at the end of a gun barrel was almost entirely at the hands of Whites. The remaining sordid and painful chronicle of the Black American (Afrodescendant) sojourn in America follows naturally from that evil beginning.

However, there is pointed evidence that all other remaining non-White people of the world (and certain recently arriving African immigrants), who have reached US shores, are also guilty of premeditated and merciless exploitation of Black Americans (Afrodescendants). Non-Blacks, who are not White, have stiff armed and stepped on the hands, backs, necks, and faces of Black Americans (Afrodescendants) as they scurried up the US socioeconomic ladder after becoming intoxicated by, and addicted to, US capitalism which is evidenced by bloodthirsty greed. Therefore, while Whites are the primary culprits up to the second half of the 20th century, other non-Blacks joined Whites thereafter in expanding and intensifying the Black American (Afrodescendant) lived hell-on-Earth existence.

This binary demarcation of parties in the Reparations fight (non-Blacks as Repairers and Blacks as Repaired) is simplifying and fortuitous. This simple and easy identification of "defendants" and "plaintiffs" makes it nearly impossible for any prospective Repairers to claim non-involvement in this tragic case. Even a cursory consultation of US economic statistics by race and ethnicity reveals immediately the clearly superior economic status of all non-Black Americans over Black Americans (Afrodescendants). Non-White non-Blacks may argue that they should not be penalized for benefitting from the "American Dream." Black

Americans' (Afrodescendants') response must be that we acknowledge certain non-Blacks' late arrival to the party. Nevertheless, they did not hesitate to join all other non-Black revelers, who gorged and drank their fill while enjoying the spectacle of continuous Black American (Afrodescendant) lynchings (aka necktie parties). The lynchings assumed many forms, but they all resulted in the unfair and injurious economic exploitation of Black Americans (Afrodescendants) that contributed to our ethnogenocide.

This brings us to a potentially disunifying issue in the Reparations fight. It was stated that the Reparations fight pits Black Americans (Afrodescendants) against all other Americans. An unquestioned reality is that citizens comprise nations, and that citizens/peoples legitimize nations through support for their governments. International law confirms that national governments are responsible/liable for "going ons" within their borders. It follows, therefore, that US governments are responsible/liable for the pantheon of egregious misdeeds and related injuries inflicted upon Black Americans (Afrodescendants). Every misdeed leveled at us during our over 400-year history in the US was sanctioned, permitted, and/or not prevented by US governments.

It is transparent that the supreme government in the US is the US Federal Government. Consequently, it is logical that the Federal Government is the most culpable party in the Black American (Afrodescendant) Reparations case. No question about it, certain governments at lower levels (state, county, municipal) are guilty of misdeeds against us. Furthermore, certain business enterprises (corporate and noncorporate), organizations and institutions, and individuals are also guilty of heinous acts against us. However, all such acts unfolded under jurisdictional authorities that, by law, are subject to the supreme governmental authority, which is always and everywhere the US Federal Government. Hence, it is logical to lodge Black Americans' (Afrodescendants') Reparations claim with the most culpable party as a starting point. It is reasonable to exhaust the process at the highest level first. Once exhausted at the highest level, then Reparations claims can be pursued at lower levels of government and with other entities that operated under the authority of those lower-level governments. Given this hierarchical approach to prosecuting the Reparations case, unfavorable outcomes at lower levels can be appealed to the supreme authority, which will have already established juridical precedents.

The concern is that the *status quo* reflects active and even completed lower-level governments' prosecution of the Black American (Afrodescendant) Reparations case, while prosecution of the case at the supreme level is yet to begin in earnest. This scenario is inconsistent with the logic expressed above and portends disagreement among Black

Americans (Afrodescendants) who prefer adherence to the top-down approach to prosecuting our Reparations case.

A transparent solution for this potential conflict is for Reparations task forces, commissions, and councils at all governmental levels to coalesce and arrive at an agreement on the most favorable strategy for prosecuting Reparations cases. Barring that, selected and the most formidable Black American (Afrodescendant) Reparations task forces, commissions, and councils should come to agree on strategic principles for engagement when prosecuting Black American (Afrodescendant) Reparation cases. Such an agreement should be offered as guidance for remaining Reparations cases.

As already noted, the Reparations case against the most culpable party has yet to begin, while the status of cases at lower levels of government spans the spectrum of stages: From uninitiated to resolved. To reconcile this situation with the preferred top-down hierarchical order for prosecuting Reparations cases, the following guidance is extended.

1. Prosecution of the Reparations case at the highest governmental level with the most culpable party should be initiated at the earliest possible point (see Chapter 7). This will be the top priority case.
2. No new formal efforts to initiate Reparations cases at lower levels of government should be undertaken until the top priority case is resolved. However, preliminary and unofficial case work can begin and continue on these lower-level cases.
3. For formal Reparations cases at lower levels of government that are ongoing, efforts should be made to suspend such cases temporarily or indefinitely until the top priority case is resolved.
4. For formal Reparations cases at lower levels of government that have been resolved, but agreed Reparations have not been dispensed, effort should be undertaken to halt Reparations delivery until the top priority case is resolved.
5. For formal Reparations cases at lower levels of government that have been resolved and Reparations have been dispensed, efforts should be undertaken to monitor the top priority case, interpret the related case results when they become available, and determine whether the results of the top priority case have significant and favorable implications for the lower-level case and whether efforts should be undertaken to pursue additional Reparations.

This guidance is intended to optimize outcomes all around using a logical and tried-and-true strategy.

The remaining business of this chapter is to inoculate Black Americans (Afrodescendants) and the public broadly against "crying towel" defenses by potential Repairers, who seek to protect and preserve their ill-gotten wealth and position of power.

There are three primary crying towel defenses that surface during Reparations discussion that are launched as reasons why Reparations should not be extended to Black Americans (Afrodescendants): (i) Reparations are debt creating/increasing; (ii) Reparations are tax increasing; and (iii) Reparations are inflation inducing.[20] Undoubtedly, there are other such defenses, but the three noted here carry strong economic overtones and are effective in raising eyebrows and motivating ears to prick up.

The following responses to these crying towel defenses are not attempts to leverage economic theory *per se* to defeat the defenses. Rather, reasonable and pragmatic responses are provided that should serve as immediate returns of fire. More in-depth theoretical responses, which have been formulated by certain scholars, will surface as Black Americans (Afrodescendants) formal Reparations cases are prosecuted.

The following are responses to the claim that Reparations will engender egregious and unsustainable debt for US governments. First, US Government debt is already unsustainable as attested by its own US Government Accountability Office and inferred by its Congressional Budget Office (CBO).[21] Second, history shows that it is possible to maintain extraordinarily high levels of debt under particular circumstances. Arguably, as long as the US Government remains the world's preeminent superpower with the largest, very vibrant, and growing economy, and can maintain sufficient investor interest in its "risk free" or "near risk free" debt securities (without intervention, using forceful threats, through soft power coercion, or otherwise), then it can manage considerably higher levels of debt than would be considered sustainable otherwise. Third, concerns about the level of debt created by Reparations may ignore the fact that the full value of Reparations that might be agreed is not likely to be extended in cash or in a one-point-in-time lumpsum payment. Fourth, Reparations are

---

[20] This topic is taken up again in Chapter 8.

[21] Government Accountability Office (2024), "The Nation's Fiscal Health: Road Map Needed to Address Projected Unsustainable Debt Levels," https://www.gao.gov/assets/d24106987.pdf; and Congressional Budget Office (2023), A letter to Congress Regarding: "CBO's Long-Term Projections of Gross Federal Debt," https://www.cbo.gov/system/files/2023-09/59512-GrossDebt.pdf (Ret. 050624).

likely to be economic growth enhancing, which means that a key debt metric (the debt-to-GDP ratio) may not be affected as dramatically or as adversely as might be first imagined. Fifth, all else being equal, Reparations will engender decreases in certain government expenditure requirements that will, in turn, reduce government deficits and the related potential growth in government debt. These five salvos should stymie this crying towel defense against Reparations.

On anticipated tax increases caused by Reparations agreements, the third, fourth, and fifth responses provided in the paragraph immediately above serve as good responses. In addition, it is important to retort that Reparations involve the righting of wrongs. Pain was inflicted on Black Americans (Afrodescendants) historically, and Reparations represent a boomeranging of that pain. In other words, non-Black Americans must expect to experience certain pain as repayment for the pain that they inflicted on us. As the saying goes: "No pain, no gain." As already discussed, Reparations certainly represent the prospect of pain for non-Black Americans, but it also creates prospects for gains for both Black and non-Black Americans. Reparations may lift the entire society to a more civil track that is not racked by the discomfort, uncertainty, and violence that is part and parcel of a society rife with racism and hate. Also, Black Americans are likely to use some of their Reparations financial assets to meet their needs. By doing so, they are likely to enrich certain non-Black Americans.

Responses concerning the inflationary effects of Reparations are as follows. First, the realization that Reparations will not be extended solely in the form of cash or as a one-point-in-time lumpsum payment reduces immediately inflationary expectation. Second, economists have shown that producers and consumers are rational and can successfully anticipate inflation and make appropriate adjustments.[22] It is unexpected inflation that disadvantages economic agents. Third, the Federal Reserve Board (FED) will be happy to hear the opinion that it has achieved a solid reputation for its ability to meet its dual mandates: Solid economic growth and low inflation. Consequently, parties that spin this crying towel defense against Reparations fail to account for the FED's prowess at preventing high and volatile inflation.

---

[22] Despite its weaknesses, the "Rational Expectations" theory that was popularized by Robert Lucas and Thomas Sargeant during the 1970s provides the stated argument. Moreover, given that current economies reflect better informed and educated agents and improved and easily available computational tools, it stands to reason that some of the arguments lodged in opposition to the theory have been deflated.

To conclude these responses to crying towel defenses and this chapter, we acknowledge that there may be no end to reasons that might surface to deny Reparations. Also, our responses to the three primary reasons for denying Reparations are not exhaustive. However, those who persist in seeking to deny Reparations should give due consideration to the following facts:

1. Reparations can serve as a healing balm that can prevent a nation from entering or continuing a destructive downward spiral that ends in a collapse.
2. Resolving Reparations claims is an undertaking with a finite time horizon. The related outflow of government resources, possible higher debt levels, higher taxes, and higher inflation that are anticipated by Reparations opposers are not likely to be permanent.
3. "Our health is our wealth." The benefits of health are generally understated, as are the adverse health effects caused by stress, crime, and violence that exist at high levels in societies that have not entertained or resolved Reparations claims.
4. The resolution of Reparations claims portends improved wellbeing for the entire society.
5. The one certain realization from written history of the known world, which is proven by our very current existence, is that humans are blessed with an unbelievable capacity to survive and adapt to even the most complex, difficult, and suddenly arising requirements to change.

Chapter 5: Reparations' Benefits and Costs

There are many reasons why economists are called the "high priests" of modern society. Largely due to economists' interventions, life has been reduced to dollars and cents. Consequently, the need to assign monetary value to all activity places economists at the center of most conversations. An important skill that is available to economists is the ability to circumscribe questions, topics, and issues for consideration to bite-size chunks so that everyone can appreciate and comprehend salient aspects of questions, topics, and issues and make relatively well-informed decisions.

For this chapter's topic, economists are most certainly required because the topic is multilayered and expansive. What benefits and costs are of concern? What is the nature of the benefits and costs (financial, physical/material, or mental)? How should benefits and costs be measured (pecuniary versus nonpecuniary)? Is the time horizon short-, medium-, or long-term? Should one be concerned with only direct, indirect, or both types of benefits and costs? Should consideration be limited to private, public, or social benefits and costs? Where should the analysis begin and end?

Before undertaking a drilling down effort to reduce the topic to a tractable size for purposes of this volume, a crucial point to consider is that the economically integrated nature of today's society means that most benefits that are enjoyed by one party often automatically translate into another party's costs—and vice versa. In other words, benefits and costs of the Reparations fight that are incurred by Black Americans (Afrodescendants) are likely to be mirrored as costs and benefits, respectively, for non-Black Americans. Please keep this in mind because what follows will be one-sided treatment of the benefits and costs to be discussed. The focus will be largely limited to benefits and costs incurred by Black Americans (Afrodescendants). Readers are invited to account for the mirrored costs and benefits to non-Blacks.

In addition, given the futuristic and conditional nature of the Reparations fight and its outcomes, it is important to remember that the benefits and costs to be incurred cannot be identified definitively. Accordingly, if economists were to seek to reduce benefits and costs to monetary terms, then they would typically apply probability measures and compute what are called "expected benefits" and "expected costs." For example, if a full Reparations payout is estimated at 100, but due to uncertainty about receiving the full payout a (judgmentally or statistically estimated) probability could be assigned. In this case, we assign a hypothetical 50.0% probability, and compute an "expected benefit" of 50 (100 * 50.0%).

In what follows, consideration of benefits and costs to be incurred by Black Americans (Afrodescendants) will be limited mainly to the most impactful or significant socioeconomic and related events; will be conceived and measured conceptually in terms of pecuniary impacts, but not explicitly identified (i.e., no monetary values will be provided); and will be understood to materialize during the period that commences today, will extend through the remaining Reparations fight, and will conclude at the point just beyond receipt of Reparations.

Important **benefits/gains** that are expected to accrue to Black Americans (Afrodescendants) from winning the Reparations fight include, but are not necessarily limited to:

1. The realization of Black Americans' (Afrodescendants') power as a people, the sanctity and power of efforts to support and endure the arduous prosecution of just causes, and increases—in untold ways—of our faith in a Universal Creator (or higher power). All of this will open to Black Americans (Afrodescendants) a boundless future. The "monkey will be thrown from our backs." The collective joy, relief, and release of stress/anxiety associated with concluding our 400 plus year journey and initiating a new journey under completely new, different, and favorable circumstances/conditions is, and will be, unmeasurable.
2. A sizeable increase (improvement in) trust, love, and unity that translate into the formation of a large positive cultural capital asset entry on the Black American (Afrodescendant) balance sheet.
3. A sizeable increase in self-esteem and a much greater sense of self-worth that will be evidenced by a deep downturn in our willingness to accept second-class citizenship status regardless of where we reside.
4. Directly connected to the previous entry (possibly just a restatement of it), Reparations will serve as a great empowering force that affects positively our inclination and motivation to involve ourselves in local, state, and national domestic affairs and in international affairs.
5. A sizeable increase in Black Americans' (Afrodescendants') independence, self-determination, self-reliance, and **liberty;** potentially evidenced by the formation of a separate government(s).
6. A huge increase in the Black Americans' (Afrodescendants') balance sheets' financial and nonfinancial assets and net worth.
7. An enormous rise in our collective and individual "stock" value around the globe and in all venues due to recognition of our unrelenting, enduring, and Herculean efforts to secure Reparations and our Jesus-like resurrection.

8. Increases and improvements in human relationships that arise from, and are directly related to, winning the Reparations fight.

Important **costs/losses** that are expected to accrue to Black Americans (Afrodescendants) from winning the Reparations fight include, but are not necessarily limited to:

1. Physical and mental injuries and deaths from official and unofficial encounters (violent attacks (including hate crimes), incarcerations, prosecutions, and murders) during and immediately following resolution of the Reparations fight.
2. Reductions in Reparations fighters' balance sheet assets (financial and/or nonfinancial) emanating from private and/or public sector retaliatory actors and actions.
3. Retaliatory denials of employment (hiring and promotions), educational, political, entrepreneurial, and other opportunities (through increased racism) within the private and public economic sectors in response to wider spread knowledge of the Reparations fight as it intensifies.
4. Increased expenditures to provide physical protection and security to those (and their property) who are threatened by the Reparations fight.
5. Increased pecuniary and psychological costs incurred to fulfill a wide range of fundamental living requirements due to expanded price discrimination (against Blacks) by non-Blacks as retaliatory responses to wider spread knowledge of the Reparations fight as it intensifies.
6. Voluntary hardships (e.g., reduced consumption, fasting, and physical training for conflicts) endured during operationalization of economic enforcement efforts to motivate and ensure receipt of Reparations (see Chapters 6 and 7).
7. The mental and physical toll of heightened stress and anxiety due to known and uncertain potentially harmful events that may be enacted by non-Blacks in response to the Reparations fight.
8. Deterioration in, or destruction of, human relationships when Reparations fight positions/sentiments conflict.
9. The legitimate leveraging of our former subaltern condition to explain shortcomings.

In his 1965 book, *The Logic of Collective Action*, noted economist and political scientist Mancur Olson revealed a simple truth: The human spirit logically/rationally seeks benefits from efforts.[23] Specifically, efforts

---

[23] Mancur Olson (1965). *The Logic of Collective Action*. Harvard University Press. Cambridge.

(individual and/or collective) are likely to be motivated and intensified the greater are the surpluses of benefits over costs associated with the efforts.

This chapter has analyzed succinctly and broadly the benefits/gains and costs/losses associated with the fight for Reparations. The magnitude and intensity of Black Americans' (Afrodescendants') efforts to secure Reparation will be determined by our assignment of (judgmental and/or estimated statistical) probabilities and our hunger and thirst for the anticipated benefits. However, Black Americans (Afrodescendants) should recognize some circularity in the Reparations calculus. Specifically, the probability of events occurring can be increased or decreased by effort levels. Accordingly, if we increase and intensify our Reparations fight efforts, then we can increase the probability of enjoying Reparations benefits. Each Black American (Afrodescendant) should examine the important and impactful benefits/gains and costs/losses identified in this chapter, factor in their own important benefits and costs if they are missing from this chapter's lists, and then perform their Reparations calculus to decide the level of effort to be offered during their Reparations fight.

If Black Americans' (Afrodescendants') testimonies about our disgust and impatience with, and hate for, the *status quo* are genuine, then the smallest surplus of benefits over costs associated with the Reparations fight should be sufficient to summon our maximum efforts. In turn, maximum efforts should increase our probability of success. If we operationalize the results of such Reparations calculus, then we should find ourselves living in a new heaven and new Earth in just a limit of time.

Chapter 6: Reparations' Requirements, Methods, and Processes

Introduction

To this point, this pocketbook has conveyed the extraordinary and unique nature of the call for Reparations by Black Americans (Afrodescendants). While individuals and small groups have experienced mixed results through their thrusts for Reparations historically, there has never been in the history of the known world the submission of a unified Reparations claim by so many, for so much, to such hard task masters and egregiously malevolent and belligerent oppressors. After all efforts have been mounted to motivate Afrodescendants to come under a unified umbrella to lodge a claim for Reparations, after all required research has been performed to substantiate and validate the case for Reparations and the claim itself, and after all negotiations are completed between offenders and claimants, there remains the possibility that offenders will experience "cold feet," will balk, and will renege on agreements/promises to make Reparation payments.

It makes no sense to plan a long and arduous journey to a palace that will provide wonderful benefits, only to find one's self at the door of the palace with the key in hand, but without the power to insert the key, turn it, hear the lock tumble to open, the door swing open, and one's eyes observe the long imagined, awaited, and beautiful environs. In other words, we must plan sufficiently to ensure that when we reach the Reparations delivery point, we can motivate (forcefully if necessary) transfer of the land, financial, material, and services resources and other assistance that are due. This chapter presents relatively high-level details of the first part of a plan that encompasses requirements and steps associated with Reparations methods and processes that move us from the *status quo* to that day when the Afrodescendant world can change favorably forever and usher in a new world order on planet Earth. Chapter 7 provides the plan's second half.

The above-mentioned requirements, methods, and processes are reflected in the following four components: (i) Coming under a unified umbrella; (ii) completing research and other efforts to substantiate and validate the case and claim for Reparations; (iii) negotiating the value and structure of the payment for the Reparations claim; and (iv) ensuring receipt of the Reparations payment. The four components are quite sequential. However, we must ensure that the process remains integrated. Most importantly, we must build capacity, tools, and power to guarantee proper fulfillment of each component. In other words, to produce Reparations, Black Americans (Afrodescendants) should prepare to invest our financial, material, and intellectual resources and to perform work that will enable the production of inputs for each of the four components according to the schedule outlined. We cannot afford supply-chain disruptions.

The current Afrodescendant Reparations effort has evolved in fits and starts over the last 35 to 40 years. We have made sporadic and idiosyncratic progress. The Reparations snowball is downhill bound. Now we must all buy into a unified vision and effort to complete the process that will grow the snowball and its speed to a size and velocity, respectively, that will not only carry us to the bottom of our final valley of despair at the foot of our current mountain, but back up the side of the adjacent mountain to its top where independence, self-determination, self-reliance, and **liberty** await us.

Unifying Under One Reparations Umbrella

In 1860, the 4.5 million US Black population was nearly monolithic. Just less than 11 percent of Blacks were "free;" the remainder were enslaved.[24] Eleven percent of a population was significant, especially when that proportion of the population served as leadership for the remainder. However, a nearly monolithic body with a small and unified head provides a much more unified model of Black Americans than we find today. As highlighted by economic and population statistics, and as summarized by *The Washington Post* Op-Ed columnist Eugene Robinson in his book, *Disintegration: The Splintering of Black America,* there are now at least four Black Americas.[25] First, there are the "super rich" by Black American standards. Second, there are so-called "middle-class" Blacks. Third there are poor Black Americans: That ~39 percent of us, who live below, at, or hover just above the poverty line and who make up most of us below the median household income level.[26] Fourth, we have Blacks who are "foreign born" mainly from the Western Hemisphere and the African Continent, who often purposely distance themselves from "native-born" Black Americans (Afrodescendants). Although it is difficult to find hard evidence concerning the proportion of Black Americans (Afrodescendants) who do or do not support the "ADOS" position on Reparations, because those deemed liable for Reparations are likely to attempt to constrain the list of

---

[24] See US Government Printing Office (1864). *Population of the United Staes in 1860: Compiled from the Original Returns of the Eighth Census*, p. ix. https://babel.hathitrust.org/cgi/pt?id=osu.32435070003405&seq=5 (Ret. 050224).

[25] Eugene Robinson (2011). *Disintegration: The Splintering of Black America*. Knopf Doubleday Publishing Group. New York.

[26] See Gloria Guzman and Meliss Kollar (2023). "Table A-2 Households by Total Money Income, Race, and Hispanic Origin of Householders: 1967 to 2022." *Income in the United States: 2022*. U.S. Department of Commerce, Bureau of the Census. https://www.census.gov/content/dam/Census/library/publications/2023/demo/p60-279.pdf (Ret. 041324).

Reparations recipients, it seems logical to adopt the position that foreign born Blacks may not to be included among recipients of Reparations receipts.[27] Therefore, we can limit our consideration to the three Black American groups arrangement. However, no matter how you twist and turn the three-groups arrangement, it is less unified, more fragmented, and more problematic than the two-groups arrangement at the Civil War's end.

What are the barriers to unification of the three Black Americas? **Realization!** All three groups—actually two of the three—should realize that we are all (to a letter) at the very bottom of the socioeconomic hierarchy in the US, and that our only way up and out is through a unified force of effort. The Black "super-rich" should realize that they are "poor rich" when compared with their non-Black counterparts. They should not deny that they were made "poor rich." While it is not very difficult to amass even a few tens of millions of dollars with a very "S-M-A-R-T" effort, one can only become a billionaire (i.e., super rich) in the US until you are "approved" to reach that lofty height.[28] To reach that status you must be useful to the real (White) super rich, and you must be committed to helping maintain and sustain the *status quo*. Deviation from that position will lead to a quick and sharp reckoning. Ask Ye (aka Kanye West) and P-Diddy (Sean Puffy Combs). The two relevant remaining Black groups (the middle-class and poor) should realize that, in the end, they will carry all the Reparations water. Why? Because the Black super rich are monitored so closely that they have constrained control over how their resources are expended and are likely to be limited in their ability to contribute significantly to any effort that countervails the *status quo*. Consequently, the poor and middle-class Black Americans (Afrodescendants) should certainly seek unification.

---

[27] The ADOS (American Descendants of Slaves) Foundation and its lead proponents, Yvette Carnell and Antonio Moore, surfaced in the middle of the second decade of the millennium as an outspoken voice on limiting Black American Reparations to descendants of those enslaved in the US. https://www.adosfoundation.org/ (041324).

[28] This acronym stands for Specific, Measurable, Achievable, Relevant, and Timebound. A SMART plan is signified by: A **specific** plan that establishes **measurable** objectives and goals to remain on a logical progress track; a plan that is not filled with delusional and/or un**achievable** objectives and goals; a plan that undergoes or conducts strategies with **relevant**/germane activities; and a plan that can produce desired results within established **timebound** constraints. Only this type of SMART economic agent can enjoy persistent success. This SMART concept can be applied to successful achievement broadly. It is attributable to Baba Asinia Lukata Chikuyu.

We venture again that this two Black American groups configuration is more fragmented than the two Black American groups arrangement at the end of the Civil War. As already noted, free Blacks were leaders for formerly enslaved Blacks after Emancipation. The former had experience navigating freedom; the latter did not. The former led and the latter followed with deference to their leaders. Today, although poor Blacks are poorly positioned economically and are somewhat dependent on publicly provided social benefits, they have a relatively high quality of life with access to many accoutrements that enable the formation of well-formed views on life and how to improve it. Therefore, they are not always willing followers. This situation is made more problematic for unification purposes with the Black middle-class group because poor Blacks can cling to the hope of wealth and success through gray market activity, the lottery, or through entertainment industries. Also, the poor have a solid grasp on a cultural lifestyle that is quite different from that in which the Black middle-class is enmeshed. Consequently, the Black poor may throw up a difference wall that separates them from their Black middle-class brothers and sisters. As you know, certain Blacks have experienced the violent wrath of other Blacks—even murdered—because of differences between those who do and do not "act White." The force of the difference between poor and middle-class Blacks is amplified by the fact that the two groups are of a similar mass. If we were to judgmentally disaggregate Black America in the following way, the size of the two groups becomes transparent: (1) Super rich = 1%; (2) middle-class = 51%; (3) poor = 39%; and (4) foreign born = 9%.[29]

Therefore, if we ignore the "super rich" and immigrant Blacks, then we are left with two groups that are somewhat similar in size and differentiated by: Sub-cultures; levels of knowledge, income, and wealth; often residing in different locations; having different aspirations and visions for life; and different opportunity sets. We should also realize that differences not only exist between middle-class and poor Blacks, but that intergroup differences prevail between the extremities of these two groups.

In accordance with the mythical Willie Lynch principles, we should realize that overt and systematic efforts have been undertaken to create and expand

---

[29] These estimates are only marginally judgmental. They are derived from two Census Bureau Sources. The first is *Op. cit.* (Guzman and Kollar, 2023). The second is The American Community Survey (2021)."Selected Characteristics of the Native- and Foreign-Born Populations." https://data.census.gov/table/ACSST1Y2021.S0501?q=S0501:%20SELECTED%20CHARACTERISTICS%20OF%20THE%20NATIVE%20AND%20FOREIGN-BORN%20POPULATIONS&g=010XX00US&tid=ACSST1Y2021.S0501 (Ret. 050224).

the aforementioned differences to serve as barriers to unification—especially unification that involves an effort to secure Reparations.

But the task before us is to unify Black Americans (Afrodescendants) for the Reparations fight. How do we achieve this outcome? Through a large volume of *Kazi* (work). As a starting point, we can hope (although this is not a strategy) for fortuitous events: e.g., crises that might galvanize us. Alternatively, we can analyze which types of crises might be most effective in helping unify middle-class and poor Blacks and then operationalize conditions that precipitate the crises. In addition, we can act logically and use prevailing leadership (legacy and non-legacy Black organizations and institutions) to engender "come to Jesus" experiences where we **REALIZE** that "we are all we got," and that if we do not act to move down the Reparations path today, then we may never have such a favorable opportunity again.

The "come to Jesus" experiences should cause most, if not all, Black American (Afrodescendant) leadership (individuals or groups) to discontinue "elite capture" because crumbs from the rich man's table will not sustain individuals or small groups operating alone. Those engaging in "elite capture" will be alienated from the larger group of Black Americans (Afrodescendants), who are not positioned to engage in such deplorable acts. The former may come to view themselves as maroons on a deserted island after larger Black groups are eliminated through drug use, incarceration and other institutionalizations, an inability to economically self-support, pandemics, patricide, etc. If prevailing Black leadership can be enabled, or enables itself, to restore their African centric communal mind and no longer adopt the self-preservationist approach to survival, then Black Americans (Afrodescendants) have a chance to unify.

What is the mechanism for forging unity? The melding of prevailing leadership with a renewed African centric and communal mind in the following types of organizations can guarantee successful unification: Religious, charitable, fraternal, educational, and social organizations. Black non-super-rich entrepreneurs must also undergo African centric communal mind renewal. This is especially true for Black entrepreneurs who have the capacity and ability to reach large numbers of Afrodescendants and influence their thinking. The latter reference is directed specifically at Black American (Afrodescendant) cultural, sports, entertainment, and media entrepreneurs. Given right-minded Black leadership we can be well on our way down a successful Reparations path.

This new Black American (Afrodescendant) leadership, which is positioned in important, Black-controlled organizations and institutions, can act to renew/transform the minds of other middle-class and poor

Blacks. Theoretically and practically, an African communal mind transformation should be well underway before proper work can be performed to implement a sound Reparations strategy.

In other words, Black Americans (Afrodescendants) **may** have already (unintentionally, of course) hamstrung or hampered our efforts to develop and implement a successful Reparations fight. Only time will confirm whether this is a valid observation. If the observation is valid, then we must find our way back to the correct path and actions. To be crystal clear about the best theoretical path to successful Reparations, we now explore how the path **should have** unfolded.

1. We should have conducted an African centric communal mind restoration campaign for Black leadership.
2. Leadership should have then conducted an African centric communal mind restoration campaign for the remainder of Black America.
3. We should have ensured the teaching and learning of ourstory in homes and schools. This would have instilled confidence and awakened the realization of our worthiness.
4. We should have developed, adopted, and performed early implementation of an overarching long-term strategic plan for Black (Afrodescendant) Americans.[30]
5. We should have accepted our oneness and purged our fear to claim our unity under a single identity and a new national umbrella.[31]

After step five was reached, then we would have achieved a sufficient level of unity and would have been prepared to launch the second component of the methods and procedures to achieve Reparations.

Validating the Case for Reparations and the Claim[32]

One can safely say that the current thrust for Black American (Afrodescendant) Reparations was inaugurated by the late U.S. Rep. John Conyers (D-MI). He introduced a Reparations Bill (H.R. 40) into the U.S.

---

[30] *Op. cit.* (Long-Term Strategic Plan Panel (2023).)

[31] The Afrodescendant Nation (ADN) is intended as a pseudo governmental entity that has made such a call. https://www.afrodescendant.org/ (Ret. 051224).

[32] Deep appreciation is extended to Kennis Henry for reviewing and contributing to this section of the chapter.

Congress in 1989.[33] That legislation and its many subsequent vintages, which have not received Congressional approval, mainly called for appointment of a commission and the provision of funds to "study Reparations requirements."

Over the past three and one-half decades, the following selected, popular, and documented milestones mark the partial unfolding of our journey to Reparations:

- Continuous refiling of H.R. 40 Bills with each subsequent Congress.
- The United Nations releases the 1993 Vienna Declaration and Programme of Action.
- President Bill Clinton apologizes on behalf of the US Government to Black American survivors of the US Government-sponsored syphilis testing program in 1997.[34]
- United Nations conducts the 2001 World Conference against Racism, Racial Discrimination, Xenophobia and Related Intolerance.
- The US Senate passed S.R. 39, which requires lawmakers to apologize to Black American lynching victims, their survivors, and their descendants in 2005.[35]
- The US House of Representatives issues an apology to Black Americans for the slavery and Jim Crow eras of the nation's history in 2008.[36]
- CARICOM's Reparatory Justice Committee Releases a 10-Point Reparations Plan in 2014.
- *Atlantic Magazine* releases Ta-Nehisi Coates' 2014 article, "The Case of Reparations."
- International Black World of the 21st Century's (IBW21's) Convenes a 2015 National/International Reparations Summit and

---

[33] See Wikipedia. "Commission to Study and Develop Reparation Proposal for African-Americans Act." https://en.wikipedia.org/wiki/Commission_to_Study_and_Develop_Reparation_P roposals_for_African- Americans_Act#:~:text=The%20%2240%22%20number%20refers%20to,40. (Ret. 050224).

[34] M4BL (Movement for Black Lives) (circa 2020). Timeline. https://m4bl.org/wp-content/uploads/2021/06/Timeline-Reparations- Now-Toolkit.pdf (Ret. 050824).

[35] Ibid. (M4BL).

[36] Ibid. (M4BL).

announces the formation of the NAARC (National African American Reparations Commission).

- The US Government agrees to pay nearly $500 million to 17 Native American Tribes for mismanagement of their resources mainly by the US Department of the Interior in 2016.
- Evanston, Illinois becomes the first US municipal government to form a Reparations Commission in 2019; it begins dispensing Reparations in 2022
- The US Congress convenes a dynamic hearing on Reparations in 2019.
- Darity and Mullen release *From Here to Equality: Reparations for Black Americans in the 21ˢᵗ Century* in 2020.
- A 2022 "Why We Can't Wait Campaign" that secured 217 Members of the US House of Representatives and 25 US Senate Members to co-sponsor Reparations legislation—the highest ever level of support.
- Reginal Muhammad releases *The National Reparations Declaration: A Qualitative and Quantitative Blueprint for Black Redress* in 2023.
- The California Legislature passes Assembly Bill 3121 that establishes a Reparations Task Force to study and develop Reparations proposals for African Americans. The Task Force issues a preliminary report in 2022 and a final report in 2023.
- Darity, Mullen, and Hubbard release *The Black Reparations Project: A Handbook for Racial Justice.*
- Beginning in October 2023 with a National Reparations Convention in Atlanta Georgia, the Afrodescendant Nation ADN) commences a series of Teach-Ins and Conventions to raise awareness and help accelerate, unify, and guide the Reparations fight.
- The State of New York approves legislation to form a Reparations Commission in December 2023, commission members are identified, and the commission work commences.

No effort is expended here to annotate or analyze the documents associated with the just-listed milestones. The documents are readily and easily available for students of Black American (Afrodescendant) Reparations to explore. However, this plan would be guilty of an embarrassing oversight if it did not, at a minimum, highlight briefly pre-1990s Reparations milestones that served as a foundation and background for the current

Reparations thrusts that were kicked off by Congressman Conyers in 1989. Consider the following scanty and selected history:[37]

- (1865) Union General William T. Shermans Special Field Order 15, which ordered that newly freed slave households be allotted "40 acres and a mule" to facilitate their proper development immediately following the Civil War. This order was later rescinded by the President Andrew Johnson Administration.
- (1866) The Southern Homestead Act permitted former Black slaves to purchase land on a noncompetitive basis.
- (1948-49) As an odd entry, we note the Nobel Prize winning role of the Black American diplomat working in the United Nations, Ralph Bunche, who helped negotiate a peace agreement between Arabs and Jews after war broke out between the two groups as the State of Israel was being established following World War II.[38]
- (1988) During Pres. Ronald Reagan's Administration, the US agreed to pay $20K each to persons of Japanese descent who experienced the horrors of life in Internment Camps during World War II in fulfillment of the "Civil Liberties Act."

While these Reparations "events" may appear sparce for a country that is nearly 250 years old, we can benefit by taking a different view concerning Reparations in the US. Harvard Kennedy School of Government scholars, Cornell Brooks and Linda Bilmes, help in this regard by clarifying that the US Government engages in Reparations payments all the time.[39] Also, if we account for the nation's evolving view about the acceptableness of Reparations as chronicled by Pew Research, then we may conclude that

---

[37] The entries that follow are generally from a list of US-related Reparations events that are presented on the Reparations4Slavery Internet portal: https://reparations4slavery.com/historical-timeline-of-reparations-payments-made/ (Ret. 041324). We extract from this list and denote here mainly those Reparations events that involve US Government involvement.

[38] Asle Sveen. "Ralph Bunche: UN Mediator in the Middle East, 1948-49." The Nobel Prize. https://www.nobelprize.org/prizes/peace/1950/bunche/article/ (Ret. 041324). Black Americans may anticipate a replication of UN intervention in our affairs.

[39] Ralph Ranalli and Susan Hughes (2022). "The United States Pays Reparations Everyday—Just Not to Black America." Harvard Kennedy School PolicyCast. https://www.hks.harvard.edu/faculty-research/policycast/us-pays-reparations-every-day-just-not-black-america#transcript-1923458 (Ret. 041324)

broad recognition of the reasonableness of extending Reparations to Black Americans may very well mature and become a dominant view.[40]

This section has provided unquestionable evidence that helps validate the claim for Black American Reparations. One can consider the documents and publications associated with Reparations milestones from the past three and one-half decades that are presented above and the sources cited within them. In addition, one can review documented evidence from earlier Reparations-related events in US history. All this information has underpinned exploding research that has produced estimates of Reparations amounts and the forms in which Reparations should be paid. It is not the goal of this plan to convince readers concerning a definitive amount or form of Reparations. Rather, it is to convey a well-considered strategy that ensures that Reparations—regardless of the amount or form(s)—are ultimately received by Black Americans (Afrodescendants). We conclude this section by acknowledging that scholarship presented in the above-mentioned sources recommends Reparation amounts ranging from a few trillion dollars to more than 20 trillion dollars (over 83 trillion dollars in one unusual case), and Reparations in various forms.

Negotiating Reparations' Value and Forms

Rightly or wrongly (only time will tell), many Black Americans (Afrodescendants) have a one-track mind on Reparations. Their mouths water over receipt of a check in the mail, or notification from their financial institution that a hefty deposit has reached their account. However, Reparations scholarship reveals that—as already noted—a considerable amount of energy and effort have gone into estimating the amount of Reparations owed and the many forms Reparations might take. In considering the latter, an important and related question arises: How should Reparations be dispensed?

On the amount, we can acknowledge that the amount is going to be huge in absolute and relative historical terms. So huge that, regardless of the amount identified, great consideration will be given by potential Repairers to the methods, procedures, and time periods over which Reparations are

---

[40] Kiana Cox and Khadijah Edwards (2022). "Reparations for Slavery." Pew Research Center. https://www.pewresearch.org/race-ethnicity/2022/08/30/black-americans-views-on-reparations-for-slavery/#:~:text=the%20country%20today.-,Most%20Black%20adults%20agree%20the%20descendants%20of%20enslaved%20people%20should,demographic%20subgroups%20of%20Black%20Americans (Ret. 041324).

dispensed. In other words, it makes no sense for Black American (Afrodescendant) or any other scholars/experts to attempt to devise a Reparations delivery strategy in isolation. After Repairers agree and commit to extending Reparations, then they must engage patiently, yet intently, with Black Americans (Afrodescendants) to ferret out amounts, procedures, and delivery methods/periods. Both Repairers and those to be Repaired must reflect considerable flexibility to hammer out a workable "deal."

Also, on the amount, many Black Americans (Afrodescendants) argue that—and rightly so—no amount is sufficient to repair completely the damage done. Returning the harmed to a state consistent with a history unaltered by European intervention on the world stage is a counterfactual that cannot be accurately imagined, envisioned, or estimated. Therefore, Reparations may always reflect a second-best reality. Nevertheless, the sheer magnitude of the pain, suffering, and inhumanity of European aggression and exploitation vis-à-vis Black Americans (Afrodescendants) has piqued the interest of innumerable researchers and motivated efforts to assign a dollar value to it. As noted in the previous section, estimates range from a few trillion dollars to well over 20 trillion dollars.

Therefore, it is important for Repairers and those to be Repaired to go into negotiations with their eyes wide open. Both sides will seek to optimize. A cold and cruel fact is that, regardless of the Reparations amount agreed— especially depending on the form(s) in which Reparations are to be dispensed—it is highly unlikely that a one-time, complete, and full lumpsum payment can be made by Repairers to those being Repaired. Fortunately, this is a resolvable potential sticking point: Repairers and those to be Repaired can agree to a sequence of monetary payments that are properly adjusted (compounded) to account for the time value of money or other resources to be offered as Reparations. Both Repairers and those to be Repaired will adopt a stiff bargaining position. However, it seems proper and right that both sides should approach negotiations with the intent of reflecting true spirits of Reparations and atonement. When the negotiations are over, agreements are reached, and Reparations are dispensed, both parties should be able to bask in a mutually mellow and warm glow knowing that the most reasonable repair was given and received, and that forgiveness (not forgetness) was given and received.

Finally, on the form(s) of Reparations, circumstances are likely to produce a Reparations package that includes the following: (i) Land; (ii) financial, materiel, and services resources; and (iii) other assistance to be provided domestically and internationally. The most difficult aspect of this component of the Reparations decision is associated with the reality with which this section began. Black American (Afrodescendant) negotiators must balance widely held expectations (even given a well-designed Reparations campaign) about Reparations in the form of a check against the long-term wellbeing of our people. On the other hand, negotiators for Repairers must balance offering financial versus nonfinancial assets, products, and services as Reparations and the related short- and long-term potential economic injury to the US. Fortunately, both sides may be able to ameliorate the concerns of those they represent by leveraging time. Unfortunately, the idea of providing Reparations over time generates risks for both sides. The bottom line is that negotiators should enter negotiations with all of this in mind and should work diligently to forge an agreement.

Ensuring Receipt of Reparations

While the American media often employs Black male thief/robber stereotypes, we do not have to function as bank robbers to ensure receipt of Reparations. However, to ensure receipt of Reparations, we must certainly plan to motivate and/or enforce desired actions by those required to extend Reparations. We must be prepared to give the same care to planning enforcement mechanisms for Reparations delivery as those engaged in planning multitrillion dollars heists. There are a few keys to our success in this regard:

1. Black Americans (Afrodescendants) should be on the same page when we operationalize enforcement actions. That is, we must be unified and working as one mind and body.
2. Black Americans (Afrodescendants) should reorient our attitudes about giving, and our proclivity to give, care and support to others even while denying our own real requirements. This mentality has been implanted fallaciously through religious teachings that countervail basic human instincts. This includes rejection of most applications of the admonition "suffering can be redemptive." If we want to continue suffering, then we should halt all efforts to obtain Reparations.
3. Black Americans (Afrodescendants) should bury our unworthiness and willingness to accept second-class citizenship. We should begin to realize that "we get what we accept." This mentality has been inbred through purposeful conditioning, but can be unlearned and expunged with proper and diligent practices.
4. Black Americans (Afrodescendants) should bury our physical and mental fears concerning Europeans (Whites). Fear, too, has been inbred through purposeful conditioning, but it, too, can be unlearned and expunged with proper and diligent practices.

If Black Americans (Afrodescendants) can be reminded concerning these important weaknesses at every turn and at every opportunity, then we can equip ourselves with the communal tools/weapons required to operationalize enforcement strategies to ensure receipt of Reparations. If we fail to do this, then we guarantee that: (i) A Reparations agreement will not be reached; or (ii) if reached, a Reparations agreement will not be fulfilled. An absence of unity, a continued willingness/proclivity to deny our own needs and accept second-class citizenship, and fear of Europeans will be sniffed out by our opposers as signs of weakness. Weakness guarantees defeat.

However, if we develop the aforementioned communal tools/weapons to enforce Reparations delivery, then our enforcement strategies will be successful. There is widespread knowledge concerning the popular saying: "America's business is doing business."[41] Therefore, the nation's vulnerability (unfavorable business/economic conditions or outcomes) is an open secret, and we should brook no delay in exploiting knowledge of that secret to ensure receipt of Reparations.

The economic enforcement strategies to which we refer are varied and multifaceted. No effort will be made to delineate the innumerable possibilities here, but the most salient and potentially impactful strategies are outlined. Importantly, there are communal mindsets that must be emphasized and adopted to enable implementation of the proposed economic enforcement strategies. For example:

1. Black Americans (Afrodescendants) should dispense with conspicuous consumption. It may be true that purchasing "bling" causes us to "shine" brightly. But it is also true that the cost of "bling" obscures us from seeing a clear picture of our own economic environment. Every dollar expended on "bling" is a dollar taken from a higher-order and more meaningfully productive use.
2. Black Americans (Afrodescendants) should begin to consume goods and services at rates consistent with our depressed incomes. The savings realized from adoption of this practice can be used to improve our wellbeing through favorable investments or through the shifting of purchases to higher-valued and more meaningful goods and/or services.
3. Black Americans (Afrodescendants) should proactively perform behavior that is effective in producing long-term wellbeing; e.g.,

---

[41] This quote is from US President Calvin Coolidge. See Ellen Terrell (2019), "When a quote is not (exactly) a quote: The Business of America is Business Edition" (January 17). https://blogs.loc.gov/inside_adams/2019/01/when-a-quote-is-not-exactly-a-quote-the-business-of-america-is-business-edition/ (Ret. 050224).

reducing or halting the consumption of products that are known to be harmful to our health. Special attention should be given to food, beverage, and sin tax goods consumption.

4. While there is no reason to reduce consumption of publicly provided services that are beneficial and safe ("safeness" is emphasized), to the extent possible and reasonable, we should revisit old family tried and true remedies for common ailments—especially when "formal and professional treatment" is not likely to produce superior outcomes and when the related treatment costs are unaffordable. Also, we should never forget that any exposure to one's opposer creates an opportunity for an attack.

Changes in the above-delineated communal mindset can produce saving that can help fortify us during difficult times that might arise during the implementation of economic enforcement strategies.

Now to selected economic enforcement strategies.[42] Please keep in mind that certain strategies that are highlighted are sound economic practices to operationalize generally, but they can take on sizeable economic significance when implemented to impose economic pain to force a Reparations agreement or the delivery of Reparations.

In simplest terms, the following economic enforcement strategies are designed to reduce semi-permanently or temporarily the stock or flow of Black American (highly liquid) financial assets to the non-Black American economy. This should reduce the earnings and profits of non-Black firms (non-corporate and corporate), slow growth of the non-Black economic sector; and reduce non-Black employment (increase non-Black unemployment). If these strategies are effective, then the expectation is that the public sector will be affected adversely through reductions in tax revenue. Also, in an effort meet one of its most important mandates, the FED may seek to accelerate growth by lowering the cost of money, which would be generally favorable for Black Americans (Afrodescendants)—to the extent there is an intent to contribute to US economic expansion.

The following economic enforcement strategies come immediately to mind; they are not exhaustive.

1. Black American (Afrodescendant) owned banks and those that are tightly linked to our areas of influence (communities) should

---

[42] The economic strategies presented are motivated, in part, by Brooks Robinson (2016), *21ˢᵗ Century Protests: A Handbook for Black America*, BlackEconomcis.org, Honolulu. https://www.BlackEconomics.org/BEAP/21CP.pdf (Ret. 041424).

make overt and frequent efforts to instill trust in their operations to attract more Black customers. Relatedly, Black American (Afrodescendant) leadership should seek to motivate/stimulate more Black banking on a semi-permanent and/or permanent basis. Of course, it is important to recognize existing capacity constraints associated with the 19 existing Black-owned commercial Black banks. (Four additional banks are known to serve Black areas of influence and reflect a Black majority Board of Directors.)[43]

2. Black American (Afrodescendant) leadership (especially religious leadership) should mount a campaign to popularize one weekday of fasting (dawn to dusk) for those above the age of 12. The practice should emphasize "no compensating consumption;" i.e., fasters should make no effort to make-up (compensate) for missed meals after fasting concludes. This practice is discipline instilling, resource saving (financial, material goods and services for producing food and performing the related cleanup, and energy), and can be health improving.

3. Black American (Afrodescendant) leadership should advocate for greater austerity in our consumption behavior.[44]

4. Black American (Afrodescendant) leadership should advocate for greater self-acceptance and love. Our preferences have been shaped largely by a White-controlled media, which has been successful in causing us to reject our natural selves. While the 1960s "I'm Black and I'm Proud" campaign moved us toward greater self-acceptance and love, some of the gain was lost subsequently. Admittedly, there has been some recovery of this mentality/spirit. However, it is being actualized by expensive practices. Simply put, Black Americans (Afrodescendants) can benefit mentally, spiritually, and financially by a return, and greater adherence, to self-acceptance and self-love.

---

[43] See Federal Deposit Insurance Corporation (2024). "Minority Depository Institution Program: MDI List." Fourth Quarter 2023. https://www.fdic.gov/regulations/resources/minority/mdi.html (Ret. 050224).

[44] Consider the following three brief submissions from Brooks Robinson. (2019) "How Black Americans Could Save Billions—Households at Least $500" (https://www.BlackEconomics.org/BEFuture/savebillions.pdf); (2023) "Black America's Consumption, Income, and Wealth" (https://www.BlackEconomics.org/BELit/ciw033123.pdf); and (2023) "Eliminating Excuses" (https://www.BlackEconomics.org/BELit/ee091523.pdf). All three submissions are from **BlackEconomics.org**. Honolulu. (Ret. 050224).

5. Black American (Afrodescendant) leadership should mount, maintain, and sustain perpetually a "Buy Black" campaign.

6. Black American (Afrodescendant) leadership should mount, maintain, and sustain "giving back" campaigns on the part of Black American (Afrodescendant) entertainment superstars who mature largely due to being ensconced in our areas of influence, but often choose to not give back at all after achieving financial success, or only giving back in ways that largely benefit the giver—not the broader area of influence (community).

7. Black American (Afrodescendant) leadership should advocate for the development of a Black American (Afrodescendant) fund to which Black Americans should contribute. The fund would serve as a resource for assisting Black Americans (Afrodescendants) who experience certain forms of distress due to no fault of their own.

8. Black American (Afrodescendant) leadership should advocate for expanded consideration of enrollment in Historically Black Colleges and Universities (HBCUs).

9. Black American (Afrodescendant) leadership should advocate for all religious and charitable organizations and households to begin acquiring at the lowest possible costs long-life storable foods to create food banks from which to draw during economic enforcement actions.

10. Black American (Afrodescendant) leadership should advocate that all Black Americans seek to form a no-cost association with available and trusted organizations/institutions in our areas of influence (communities), and that those organizations/institutions begin to plan for economic enforcement actions in the form of short- and long-term withdrawals, work stoppages, boycotts, etc. Fundamental to such arrangements would be the formation of communication networks of members to inform them about, and during, these economic enforcement actions.

11. Black American (Afrodescendant) leadership should motivate relevant organizations/institutions to perform research and share the related results concerning conditions under which Black Americans (Afrodescendants) can legitimately withhold (yet place in trust accounts) property tax payments (and potentially municipal fees and other charges) in response to local municipalities' failures to provide services that are due.

12. Black American (Afrodescendant) leadership should advocate that large municipalities with actual or near Black (Afrodescendant) majority populations consider examining and revising, to the extent legally possible, current post-employment benefit programs that are available to former employees, who may have engaged, in a significant way, in employment discrimination

against Black Americans (Afrodescendants) in hiring, firing, and promotions. This is a particularly meaningful area for action because those formerly in control of certain large municipalities that are led currently by Black Americans (Afrodescendants) delayed in modifying the post-employment benefit programs to their advantage (i.e., there were purposeful and significant delays in transforming post-employment benefit programs from defined benefit to complete or partial defined contribution programs). The saving generated by revising benefits delivered under these programs will be associated with significant reductions in expenditures. The saving could be redirected to benefit current residents of municipalities. Note that former employees of these municipalities may have migrated to the sunbelt or elsewhere, and the municipalities receive almost no benefit from these former employees who pay no taxes to the municipalities.[45]

13. Black American (Afrodescendant) leadership should advocate that Black youth, who are searching for career opportunities, give due consideration to the "Ali Case" before committing to short-term or career employment in US military forces.

These economic enforcement strategies are sound, they can inflict pinpoint economic injury on our opposers, and they can direct pinpoint economic benefits to Black Americans. When prepared for, planned, and executed properly and in unity, these strategies can guarantee our success in applying pressure to our opposers, thereby motivating them to act as desired. Otherwise, we can ensure that they feel the economic pain that we impose.

But accounting for less than 14% of the US population, Black Americans (Afrodescendants) should realize that we may also require assistance from other quarters to secure Reparations. As a strategic reminder, consider that the US and global economies are based on "trust." The dollar bill signals this fact with the motto: "In God We Trust." Your employer trusts you to work professionally and diligently; your mortgage and car loan companies trust that you will labor, earn income, and repay your debt; and, yes, US governments (all levels) expect you to pay your taxes, fines, fees, etc. Trust is the balancing point on which the "house of cards" rests. If economic agents lose trust, then the system is done. Consequently, it may become important—even necessary—to engender a reduction in the trust invested in the system as part of a Reparations enforcement strategy.

---

[45] See Brooks Robinson (2023). "Providing Retirement Benefits for Descendants of Former Slave Master" BlackEconomics.org. https://www.BlackEconomics.org/BELit/prbfdofsm081123.pdf (Ret. 050224).

Given these enforcement strategies, we present a strategic action plan in the next chapter that outlines when and where enforcement actions may be required as part of the Reparations fight.

Chapter 7: A Strategic Plan for Securing Reparations

This chapter leverages the foregoing chapters to envision and craft a series of strategic actions that can transport Black Americans (Afrodescendants) from today's *status quo* to receipt of Reparations. The plan uses the conceptual framework from, expands on, and operationalizes an idea popularized by long-time Reparations warrior, Kamm Howard, which features a political pathway for securing Reparations. It integrates grassroots organization, with high-level politics, and media, economic, and public administration efforts. It can assist us with not "passing a bar" that has separated us from full first-class citizenship in America, but with capturing "BAR" (Black American (Afrodescendant) Reparations).

The strategic actions outlined below are systematic and specific, but they are not overly precise. Implementers of this strategy will enjoy the authority and flexibility of developing and implementing actions with the precision required to meet time and circumstantial factors that are not transparent now. Also, the strategy can be viewed as a roadmap that is used when and as needed. That is, if the strategy presented here is not adopted now, then it may be modified and adopted in the future. Also, if the strategy is operationalized and is not fully successful, then it can be revised and re-operationalized at a future point.

A favorable confluence of events is emerging. Consequently, it may be in Black Americans' (Afrodescendants') best interest to move with some urgency to capture benefits made available by these events. Some may argue that "haste makes waste." We invite harborers of those sentiments to remember that: "When the Lord gets ready, you got to move." Also, consider that angels did not visit Lot and his family for an elongated stay, but with an urgent message: (paraphrasing) "Before the sun rises, be on your way." It could be that those who are reticent to move/act now may come to comprehend the nature of a pillar of salt.

There is the wise saying: "God helps those who help themselves." Hence, we should view today as a great opportunity to receive grace offered by the Universal Creator by allowing current circumstances to motivate us to perform actions that will open the way forward to our desired and divine destination.

We have all been educated concerning "House vs. Field Negroes." Also, we have over 400 years of history concerning how Black American plans for liberation were disrupted or thwarted by those who slipped away to warn "old master." Not to worry. This plan is out in broad daylight. Everyone can come to know its content. We do not need an element of surprise. What we need is righteousness and a truthful commitment to our cause. While we do not know what might visit those who do not operate in righteousness and truth as this plan is operationalized, we do know that: "The light is on; the Creator is present in the darkness and in the light; What was and is intended for evil will be transformed for our good; 'God plans and man plans—God is the best of planners;' and 'we are gods...'"

Table 1 presents a Black American (Afrodescendant) Reparations strategic action plan for consideration.

Table 1.--Black American (Afrodescendant) Reparations: Strategic Action Plan: 2024-2029[46]

Line No.	Periods	Black Americans (Repaired)	Black American (Afrodescendant) Leadership	Prospective Repairers
1	By 053124	Participate in ADN-sponsored Washington, DC Convention	ADN, LFNOI, and NOI form collaborative relationships and launch a joint appeal to legacy Civil Rights organizations (NAACP, NUL, NAN), CNBC, ITC-represented denominations, Divine Nine Organizations, CBC, NEA (1 & 2), NMA, NBA, IBW21 (NAARC), selected Black Media operations, and representatives from selected state and local government Reparations Commissions and Task Forces to form a National Reparations Council (NRC).	
2	By 063024	Kept informed of developments by NRC; recipients of ongoing efforts by NRC members and other Black (Afrodescendant) organizations and institutions to improve our wellbeing.	The NRC forms an agreement using this plan as a starting point (required refinements are adopted); finalize requirements for a Reparations Proposal for political parties; designate officials present NRC requests for adoption of a Reparations proposal during July and August political conventions. [The NRC should request a commitment from presidential candidates and parties to approve—by any means necessary—the first of two new Reparations Bills (or use an Executive Order) during first 90-days of the 2025-29 presidential administration.] The first of the two new Reparations Bills (to be prepared by the CBC and the NRC) should call for establishment of a Reparations Commission (RC) within the first 180 days of the 2025-28 administration to utilize extant research to produce Reparations details (estimated amounts, forms, and delivery periods). The bill would extend special powers to the RC to conduct priority engagements with all relevant US Government agencies (e.g., OMB, CBO, Treasury, Interior, Justice, etc.) to fulfill its mandate. Results of the RC's efforts would serve as content for the second Reparations Bill. The RC would function under a special (select) congressional committee and be authorized to operate for 18 months. The NRC would have advisory status for selection of RC members and RC operations. The agreement should require that presidential candidates and their parties agree to use all means necessary to ensure passage of the second Reparations Bill during months 25- 42 of the presidential administration.	Presidential candidates and Political Parties (Repubs and Dems) receive the NRC's proposal during their summer 2024 conventions.

---

[46] These are the full forms of acronyms used in this table: ADN-Afrodescendant Nation; CBC-Congressional Black Caucus; IBW21-Institute of the Black World 21ˢᵗ Century; ITC-Interdenominational Theological Center; LFNOI-Lost Found Nation of Islam; NAACP-National Association for the Advancement of Colored People; NAARC-National African American Reparations Commission; NAN-National Action network; NBA-National Bar Association; NEA1- National Economic Association; NEA2-National Education Association; NMA-National Medical Association; NRC-National Reparations Council; NUL-National Urban League; OMB-Office of Management and Budget; and RC-Reparations Commission.

Line No.	Periods	Black Americans (Repaired)	Black American (Afrodescendant) Leadership	Prospective Repairers
3	By 083124	Ditto and receive recommendations from the NRC concerning the choice candidate	NRC assess presidential candidates' and parties' responses to its Reparations Proposal and determines the candidate and party to recommend to Black Americans (Afrodescendants) for the November 2024 elections. If Dem or Rep presidential candidates and parties fail to agree to NRC's Reparational Proposal, then the NRC should recommend a third-party candidate to Black Americans (Afrodescendants)	Presidential candidates and parties respond to NRC's Reparations Proposal
4	By 113024	Vote prolifically as recommended by the NRC during the November 2024 elections	NRC members vigorously support the chosen candidate for the 2024 Presidential election among their constituents and prepare to identify and appoint RC members. If Dem or Rep presidential candidates and parties fail to agree to the NRC's Reparations Proposal, then the NRC should commence preparing an appropriate response(s).(enforcement actions).	Presidential candidates and parties begin planning to implement NRC Proposal.
5	By 033125	Recipients and beneficiaries of ongoing NRC and other efforts.	If Dem or Rep presidential candidates and parties fail to agree to NRC's Reparational Proposal, then the NRC should request development of a broad strategic response (economic enforcement actions) by NRC members and their constituents. Otherwise, monitor and manage agreement.	First Reparations Bill Approved/Executive Order Issued
6	By 063025	Recipients and beneficiaries of ongoing NRC and other efforts; and implement strategic responses.	If Dem or Rep presidential candidates and parties fail to agree to NRC's Reparational Proposal, then the NRC should receive strategic responses (economic enforcement actions), reach agreement concerning implementation of strategic responses by Black Americans (Afrodescendants), and order the onset of implementation of strategic responses. Otherwise monitor and manage agreement.	RC operations commence
7	By 123126	Recipients and beneficiaries of ongoing NRC and other efforts; and implement strategic responses.	If Dem or Rep presidential candidates and parties fail to agree to NRC's Reparational Proposal, then the NRC should assess the impact and efficacy of strategic responses (economic enforcement actions) and make necessary modifications to strategic responses. Otherwise monitor and manage agreement	RC completes its mandate and second Reparations Bill prepared
8	By 063028	Recipients and beneficiaries of ongoing NRC and other efforts; and implement strategic responses.	If Dem or Rep presidential candidates and parties fail to agree to the NRC's Reparations Proposal, then the NRC should assess the impact and efficacy of the ongoing strategic responses (economic enforcement actions) and make necessary modifications to strategic responses. Also, the NRC should use Black Americans' (Afrodescendants) sentiments as a barometer to determine whether this strategic action plan should be recycled Otherwise monitor and manage agreement	Second Reparations Bill Approved/Executive Order Issued

Line No.	Periods	Black Americans (Repaired)	Black American (Afrodescendant) Leadership	Prospective Repairers
9	By 123128	Recipients and beneficiaries of ongoing NRC and other efforts.	If the second Reparations Bill is approved, then the NRC should establish methods and procedures for ensuring that Repairers develop proper policies and procedures for bill implementation. Otherwise, an appropriately modified NRC Reparations Proposal should be operationalized.	Implementation of second Reparations Bill
10	By 033129	Recipients and beneficiaries of ongoing NRC and other efforts; and implement strategic responses.	If the second Reparations Bill is approved, then the NRC should monitor bill implementation to identify issues/concerns. The NRC should call for its members to develop appropriate strategic responses (economic enforcement actions) to failure to properly implement the second Reparations Bill. Otherwise, an appropriately modified NRC Reparations proposal should be operationalized.	Implementation of second Reparations Bill
11	By 063029	Recipients and beneficiaries of ongoing NRC and other efforts; and implement strategic responses.	If the second Reparations Bill is approved, then the NRC should monitor bill implementation to identify issues/concerns. Also, the NRC should approve, and order implementation of, strategic responses (economic enforcement actions) developed by its members if issues/concerns arise with implementation of the second Reparations Bill. Otherwise, an appropriately modified NRC Reparations proposal should be operationalized.	Implementation of second Reparations Bill

Source: BlackEconomics.org analysis.

Although this strategic action plan reflects a five-year duration, it may serve as a framework for a more elongated and detailed strategic plan according to Black Americans' (Afrodescendants') evolving needs.

This is the most essential, critical, and novel chapter of this plan to secure Reparations. It may very well be the first plan to specify a date by which Black Americans (Afrodescendants) expect to receive Reparations. It certainly provides a very optimistic date.

However, we live in interesting times with the world shifting and producing inflexion points frequently. The pace of change is mercurial. Therefore, we cannot expect to continue ambling along nonchalantly and hope to stumble upon Reparations. To the extent that we can, we should take charge of our destiny and act to realize outcomes about which we have fantasized and can produce. If we want something new, then we must do and be something new under the sun.

Chapter 8: A Novel Reparations Payment Strategy[46]

In the best of all worlds, Black Americans (Afrodescendants) convince a majority of Americans that Reparations should be the order of the day. Enough support may form and concerns that serve as the most important final hurdles before the finish line are: How will the US Government pay Reparations because such a payment is likely to be tax increasing, debt expanding, and inflation inducing.[47] Opposers may argue against extending Reparations using economic principles that support their reasoning. However, the application of economic principles without full knowledge of conditions and relevant data can cause errors in policymaking. This chapter brings Reparations opposers and advocates into the light seldom-considered realities.

It is important to note that economist advocates for Reparations often dismiss Reparations opposers, who push back on the idea for the reasons given, by appealing to the following selected and popular arguments: (1) Modern Monetary Theory (MMT);[48] and (2) US Government expansive crisis spending (e.g., spending during the Great Recession of 2008/9 and the Covid-19 Pandemic of 2020-22).

Those arguments are left behind and keys are sought, not under the light post, but in the bowels of US Government operations. Specifically, the US Government Accountability Office (GAO) reports to the US Congress that seldom reach the public's eyes and ears. Did you know that the US Government is a crime victim, and that it lacks certain proficiencies? When the bite has been taken out of the crimes against the US Government and when government's proficiencies are improved, then a significant source of funds for Reparations should surface that will dispel concerns about the taxes, debt, and inflation increasing effects of Reparations.

The GAO estimated that during fiscal years (FYs) 2018-2022, which includes massive Covid-19-related government spending, the value of

---

[46] This chapter is an adaptation of Brooks Robinson (2024), "Can Crime Pay the Black American (Afrodescendant) Reparations Bill?" BlackEconomics.org.
https://www.blackeconomics.org/BELit/ccptbarb042624.pdf (Ret. 051224).

[47] A partial discussion of this topic appears in Chapter 4.

[48] MMT posits that the vagaries of inflation serve as the primary constraint to monetary expansion. That is, governments can and should adopt expansionary monetary policies that should only be altered when the related inflationary effects become troublesome.

annual fraudulent transactions was between $233 billion and $521 billion.[49] For FY 2023, GAO reported that the value of identified improper payments (i.e., monetary transactions that were executed improperly) was $236 billion; the GAO hastened to add that the just-given value was not comprehensive.[50] Given that the just-reported fraudulent transactions and improper payments estimates are not overlapping, and with the former representing an "exceptional (Covid-19)" period and the latter not being comprehensive, neither estimate is fully satisfying. Consequently, we suggest that it is reasonable to conclude that the combination of fraudulent and improper payments typically account for about five percent (**5.0%**) of all US Government expenditures.[51]

To determine potential sources of revenue to support Reparations payment, the following question is ignored: Are the above-cited fraudulent transactions and improper payments recoverable? Also, although the creativity of criminals may be prolific, we anticipate that the gap will close between the rate at which technology and artificial intelligence (AI) grow to detect and prevent crime and the rate at which criminals devise new strategies for committing crimes. Given a concerted US Government effort to employ all available technologies to stifle leakage of funds, imagine that the value of fraudulent transactions and improper payments are reduced by 80% to 90% in the medium term. Therefore, using FY 2023 as a case study, it is reasonable to estimates that fraudulent transactions and improper payments are reduced from $350 billion under today's conditions to just the $35-to-$70 billion range after crime prevention expertise is increased substantially.

[The $350 billion amount is computed as ~$7 trillion in total US Government expenditures for FY 2023 multiplied by **5.0%**, which is the current expected loss rate due to fraudulent transactions and improper payments that was established above.[52] The $35 and $70 billion amounts

---

[49] Government Accountability Office (2024A), *Fraud Risk Management: 2018-2022 Data Show Federal Government Losses an Estimated $233 Billion to $521 Billion Annual to Fraud, Based on Various Risk Environments.* https://www.gao.gov/assets/d24105833.pdf (Ret. 042424).
[50] Government Accountability Office (2024B), "Improper Payments: Information on Agencies' Fiscal Year 2023 Estimates." https://www.gao.gov/assets/d24106927.pdf (Ret. 042424).
[51] The 5.0% estimate is at the top of the range of such estimates identified through studies of other governments' losses: The range is from 0.5% to 5.0%. *Op cit.* (GAO 2024A), p. 18.
[52] The ~ $7.0 trillion is from BEA's National Income and Product Account Table 3.2 Federal Government Current Receipts and Expenditures, line 43. www.BEA.gov (Ret. 042424).

are computed by multiplying the $350 billion amount by 0.5% and 1.0%, respectively, which represent 90% and 80% **reductions** in the current expected loss rate (**5.0%**), respectively.]

In other words, if the US Government engineers substantial reductions in leakages from the system (i.e., by 80%-to-90%), then it would generate $280-to-$315 billion in saving; i.e., $350 billion less the above-referenced $70 and $35 billion in fraudulent transactions and improper payments. This $280-to-$315 billion should be viewed as potential saving that could finance Reparations. For convenience in completing this analysis, $300 billion is estimated judgmentally as saving for Reparations.

Additional saving for Reparations should come from US Government cost efficiency gains. The GAO developed a series of reports for the US Congress during 2011 to 2023 that included 1,753 recommendations designed to assist Federal Government agencies in eliminating, reducing, or better managing fragmentation, overlap, or duplication in operations and in achieving cost saving or enhancing revenue. These recommendations produced financial benefits totaling ~$600 billion.[53] Consequently, the 12-year effort produced about $50 billion in annual saving or new revenue.

The $300 billion saving from reduced losses due to fraudulent transactions and improper payments plus the just cited $50 billion in efficiency gains combine to generate $350 billion in savings for Reparations. Now account for expanding budgets due to economic growth and increased expertise in squeezing these types of saving from budgets, and it would not be unexpected that ~$400 billion could be available annually for Reparations for Black Americans (Afrodescendants) in the medium term.

But this very favorable scenario does not end here. It is true that $400 billion would be just a fraction of the Reparations bill that has been estimated at $10-to-$14 trillion.[54] However, these two estimates present a very tractable **hypothetical** problem. Consider the following strategy as a **hypothetical** solution for funding Reparations:

---

[53] Government Accountability Office (2023)."Government Efficiency and Effectiveness: Opportunities to Reduce Fragmentation, Overlap, and Duplication and Achieve Billions of Dollars in Financial Benefits; p.1. https://www.gao.gov/products/gao-23-106864 (Ret. 042524).

[54] Noted expert on Reparations for Black Americans, Duke University Professor William Darity, Jr., has suggested this Reparations amount while engaged in public discourses on the topic.

- The final Reparations bill is negotiated to the midpoint of the Reparations range amount ($10-to-$14 trillion) mentioned above—$12 trillion.
- Multiform Reparations are extended to Black Americans (Afrodescendants): i.e., land; financial and material resources; service provision agreements; and international support.[55]
- All Reparations forms except financial resources are configured to account for say one-half of the total negotiated Reparations amount—$6 trillion.
- Given a $6 trillion cash Reparations requirement (financial resources) and $400 billion in annually available Reparations funds, an agreement should be reachable in the form of a series of 15 payments. Of course, the $6 trillion and $400 billion should be adjusted to account for the time value of money at an agreed interest rate.

However, there is one remaining piece of the funding Reparations puzzle; i.e., funding that can generate the saving that was just identified. The GAO has advised that when nonproficient aspects of US Government operations are made more proficient (i.e., modifying procedures to meet current production requirements at lower costs), then savings can materialize. No doubt, increased use of new technologies will facilitate generation of these savings.

At the same time, there are additional cost efficiency enhancing methods that can employ human efforts and technologies to perform surgical-like identification and removal of "operational fat." As one tangible example, consider the US Government expenditures to collect, analyze, and disseminate statistics. Presumably, these statistics are (were) required for effective decision making. However, the economy evolves perpetually. Therefore, efforts (human and technological) should be made to track the usefulness of the statistics that are produced and the reports and databases in which they are presented. Statistics and related reports that do not reflect sufficient utilization should be discontinued.

Other vantage points from which the usefulness of statistics can be assessed include their timeliness, quality, and their impact. To clarify, certain statistics that cannot be collected, analyzed, and disseminated in a very timely manner may have limited operational usefulness today, but they may

---

[55] Our vision for multiform Reparations appears in Brooks Robinson (2015), "A Broad Three-Point Reparations Program for US Afrodescendants Versus CARICOM's 10-Point Program," BlackEconomics.org. https://www.BlackEconomics.org/BELit/btprp.pdf (Ret. 042524).

have constituted a sole source of such statistics when their collection was initiated. Obviously, these statistics should be discontinued.

The production of high-quality statistics may be a very costly undertaking. Consequently, a relatively poor-quality version of such statistics may be collected because, at some past point, the poor-quality statistics were available at a relatively low cost, and access to the poor-quality statistics was better than not having the statistics at all. Unless the latter condition remains, then these statistics should be eliminated or newly available cheaper methods should be employed to collect them or improved statistics that are now available.

By impact of statistics is meant that they assist in generating a preferred outcome. For example, statistics may be collected to serve as inputs for a statistical model that is used to guide decision making. However, an assessment of the effectiveness or accuracy of the decisions made using the statistical model's results may reveal that the model is not as effective as desired for the following types of non-exhaustive reasons:

1. Changed conditions have made the model ineffective in guiding decision making.
2. The model's underlying statistics are of insufficient quality to improve the model's results, which would improve decision making.
3. Related to 2, the occurrence(s) that is (are) measured and reflected in the statistics changed and have rendered the statistics irrelevant for the model.

In addition, although certain statistics may have been integral to past model effectiveness, an assessment of models and their underlying statistics may reveal that model effectiveness is neither hurt not helped by the inclusion or exclusion of certain statistics. In all these scenarios, the statistics' impacts are reduced and signal that their collection, analysis, and dissemination should be halted.

Available technologies should be sufficient to identify all these scenarios and flag statistics for discontinuation, which can produce significant saving. For FY 2023, the US Government expended at least $3 billion in support of its wide-ranging set of statistical programs. It may be possible to squeeze 10%-to-15% of total expenditures out of these programs on a periodic basis. These savings could, in turn, be used to fund the human expertise, hardware, and software required to perform the efforts described earlier in this chapter that can reduce substantially fraudulent transactions and improper payments.[56]

This chapter has presented realistic conditions under which Reparations can be extended by the US Government to Black Americans (Afrodescendants) without the often cited and problematic downsides that opposers argue will accompany Reparations: Increased taxes, expanded Federal Government debt, and worrisome inflation. Also, it is absent a need to appeal to MMT or recent adverse economic events that forced extraordinary levels of government spending to rescue a nation in crisis.

The scenario outlined here is akin to religious and mythical accounts where there is an intent to perform a good deed, but there is no wherewithal to do so. But sudden and magical events make resources available with which to perform the good deed. Afterward the do-gooder is rewarded.

The Black American (Afrodescendant) Ourstory that produced the current Reparations demand can never countenance the US Government as a do-gooder. Fortunately, justice requires that all paths that may produce a modicum of redemption for the US Government and the larger nation must traverse its balance sheet and reduce its value significantly.

---

[56] This discussion of US Government statistics programs as a potential source of saving is derived from Brooks Robinson (2024), "Can Statistics Help Pay the Black American (Afrodescendant) Reparations Bill?" BlackEconomics.org. https://www.BlackEconomics.org/BELit/cshptbarb050324.pdf (Ret.050424).

Chapter 9: Conclusion

This pocketbook reflects a somewhat hurried, yet systematic, effort to ensure against a reduction in the Black American (Afrodescendant) Reparations momentum and to reinvigorate the fight. Its most important contributions to the Reparations literature are: (i) It is prepared for the Reparations laity; (ii) it can serve as a handy reference on Reparations; (iii) it urges urgency in prosecuting the Reparations fight; and (iv) it offers a new and very mutually favorable strategy for paying the Reparations claim.

History has created—for good reasons—the adage: "Strike while the iron is hot." There is a current upsurge of interest among Black (Afrodescendant) people throughout Africa and the African Diaspora in securing Reparations. At the same time, there are threats that can widen existing wars around the globe. Leaders of the Reparations Movement should plan to: (i) Accelerate the fight to win Reparations before a large-scale global war erupts; (ii) use the public's preoccupation with, and the distractions produced by, a widespread and large-scale war to engineer a "quiet" Reparations agreement; or (iii) ride the wave of a widespread war and the uncertainty and change that it produces to position strategically to win Reparation during, but most likely after, the war.

World War III or not, it is logical for Afrodescendants to intensify the Reparations fight. The lightening-speed global pace of change for our opposers is expanding socioeconomic gaps between Black and Whites and, in certain cases, between Blacks and non-Blacks broadly. Time delays in decision making about improving the wellbeing of Blacks versus non-Blacks could very well serve to widen gaps further. It is unacceptable that Afrodescendants around the globe are strung along with stated or unstated promises or hints that gaps will be narrowed—not closed—in the future. It is well understood that Afrodescendant nations and peoples continue to operate as cooperative agents in the global economy mainly because of these promises and hints. Undoubtedly, we would become less cooperative if we knew with certainty the outcomes that our opposers have planned for us.

We can obtain information about, learn, and even know with certainty our opposers' plans concerning Reparations by pressing the Reparations fight and forcing "Yes" or "No" decisions. "Yes" decisions are preferred, but "No" decisions are not completely unfavorable. "No" decisions are clear signals to Afrodescendants that our existing strategies for elevating our wellbeing are inadequate. "No" decisions will motivate us to devise new, direct, and more effective strategies that bypass efforts to deny Reparations. The strategies should embody certain "Takeconomics" principles consistent with those leveled at Afrodescendants by Whites after the latter emerged from Europe to conquer the world over 500 years ago. The sooner we force a Reparations decision, the more time we will have to enjoy Reparations, or to formulate and execute alternate strategies that will optimize our future wellbeing.

We have made every effort to give our opposers no way out. The novel strategy that we propose for paying the Reparations claim can be viewed as a godsend for our opposers and a work of faith for us that "a way will be made out of no way." The US Government's own reports reveal that Reparations can be financed with funds realized by reducing crime and inefficiencies in its operations. These actions will open the way for extending Reparations without increased taxes, expanded debt, or higher inflation. While this may appear too good to be true, the evidence speaks for itself. What Black (Afrodescendant) Americans need to capture Reparations is for the US Government to: (i) Apply its "Law and Order" philosophy to crimes against itself by employing the most up-to-date and supreme crime deterring technologies (the US Government is notorious for applying these principles to Black American petty criminals); (ii) continue reducing operational inefficiencies; and (iii) to reduce spending in areas where the work being performed currently does not add favorably and/or materially to outcomes. Saving derived from these strategies are likely to be more than sufficient to fund Reparations for Black Americans (Afrodescendants).

This pocketbook's early and brief chapters provide fundamental information about Reparations in new ways. Reparations are defined. Explanations are offered concerning why Black Americans (Afrodescendants) should engage in the Reparations fight. The *Capoeira*-like engagement between a multilayered set of Repairers and those to be Repaired is discussed, and suggestions are offered concerning the most favorable strategic sequence for prosecuting the fight. Guidance is provided concerning the Reparations calculus that Black Americans (Afrodescendants) individually and collectively should perform to decide the effort levels that should be exerted in the Reparations fight.

Chapters 6 and 7 should sharpen acuity concerning Black Americans' (Afrodescendants') path to receipt of Reparations. Chapter 6 discusses the strategic components that are required and how to employ them to prosecute the Reparations fight successfully. Chapter 7 provides a related time bound strategic action plan. Scrutiny of the path outlined in this two-chapter plan to secure Reparation reveals that it is structured to yield results in the near- to medium-term, but it can be modified and elongated easily.

A noteworthy point about the plan presented in Chapters 6 and 7 is that implementing it "as is" may expose a weakness. The plan calls for a hurried forging of unity among important Black American (Afrodescendant) leadership groups just before entering the Reparations fight full force.

Typically, unbreakable unity is forged through bonds of extended duration. However, the following two outcomes are likely when the plan is implemented—both are favorable. On the one hand, opposers' efforts to create disunity among Black American (Afrodescendant) leadership groups could and should spark an intensification of efforts among the groups to strengthen unity and increase chances for success. On the other hand, whether an absence of perfect unity or any other factor precipitates an unsuccessful initial Reparations thrust, the plan can be revised and elongated, any flaws identified can be corrected, and a revised plan can be reinitiated with elevated prospect for success. Full knowledge of this should guide the provision of information about, and promulgation of, this plan.

Chapter 8 reveals the main link that is often missing from the chain that connects the Reparations demand to Reparations receipt. A sizeable group within a nation, which reflects the most inhumane history in the world, claims that Reparations cannot be extended to the most deserving of recipients ever using the excuse that resources are unavailable. Chapter 8 shows that "there is no truth in that lie."[57] If the nation continues to use this argument, then it will sound its own death knell as prospects for peaceful racial/ethnic coexistence will evaporate.

It has taken over 400 years for Black Americans (Afrodescendants) to: (i) Awaken to the reality that we have always been at war in this land; (ii) recognize that we cannot win a shooting war and capture enough booty to compensate ourselves for our troubles, pain, suffering, and deaths; and (iii) decide that pursuit of Reparations is our best strategy for capturing at least partial justice for the unspeakable injustices rained upon us.

Without doubt, sane people around the world with just a passing knowledge of US History—even in its most sugar-coated form—agree that Reparations are past due to Black Americans (Afrodescendants). Yet stalling and delaying tactics abound by the greedy, who seek to protect and preserve the wealth and power position they obtained illegally and inhumanely. But time is winding up and out. Nevertheless, certain Black Americans (Afrodescendants) will choose to sit, watch, pray, wait, and expect justice to be produced by the late Rev. Dr. Martin Luther King's eloquent reminder: "The moral arc of the universe is long, but it bends toward justice." However, other Black Americans (Afrodescendants) will

---

[57] This is a saying from a wise communal mother, Maude Johnson, from the author's formative years.

adopt a different posture. We will perform (may have already performed) the Reparations calculus discussed herein and decide to exert maximum effort in the fight to secure Reparations—as the late Malcom X (aka El-Hajj Malik el-Shabazz) advised—"by any means necessary."

Given "made up minds" concerning Reparations, there is no power on Earth that can stop Black Americans (Afrodescendants) from achieving the righteous goal of securing Reparations to heal ourselves, our descendants, and our lands.

About the Author

Dr. Books Robinson is a graduate of the University of Wisconsin-Madison (bachelor's degree) and of George Mason University in Fairfax, Virginia (master's and doctoral degrees). He now serves as the Chief Contributor for an over 18-year-old Internet website that he founded, BlackEconomics.org, and as an economic consultant. He has over 30 years of domestic and international experience as an economist in the public and private sectors covering the following topics: National and public sector economic accounting, innovation, economic development in Asia, and on Black American and ethnic economic issues. His written submissions span a wide range of economic topics. Most of his written and recorded submissions are available on the BlackEconomics.org website. Most of his early submissions appear on the National Center for Public Policy Research website; https://nationalcenter.org/ncppr/staff/b-b-robinson-ph-d/.

He is well known for fresh and unique perspectives delivered through social criticisms and analyses of economic topics.

BBR:052024